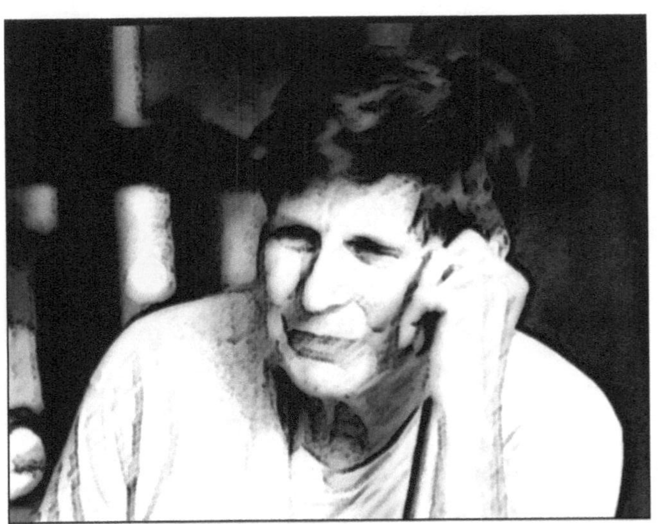

"We need to share our words for power,
so also do we need to share the contours
of our faces, and the visual shapes
of our lives."

—Audre Lorde

Black Silk and Other Poems

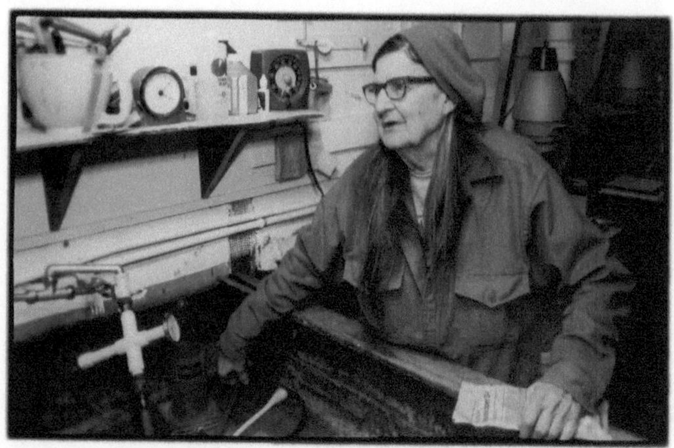

*Ruth Mountaingrove in the Ink People photography darkroom
printing "Drawings with Light"*

Previously Published & Exhibited Work

Poetry Collection, *Rhythms of Spring,* (as Ruth Elizabeth Shook, at 23 years old) Huffnagle Press, New Hope, PA 1946.

Contributor, *Approach* No. 13, Rosemont PA 1954.

Contributor, *Women, A Journal of Liberation* "In the Arts" Issue, Fall, 1970.

Contributor, *aphra,* a feminist literary magazine, Vol. 2, No. 3, summer 1971 (contributor since1968).

Photographs, *Ask No Man Pardon,* pamphlet, Elsa Gidlow, Druid Heights Books, 1973.

Founder, Editor & Contributor, *WomanSpirit Magazine,* published quarterly by Ruth and Jean Mountaingrove, Rootworks, Southern Oregon, a radical feminist commune, Vol. 1, No. 1, Autumn Equinox, 1974 (to 1984).

Songbook and original music, *Turned On Woman,* New Woman Press, Wolf Creek, Oregon, April, 1975.

Contributor, *BookLegger Magazine* Vol. 2, No. 11 Bumpkin Press, San Francisco, CA. (Published by/for Library Workers) Sept./Oct. 1975.

Contributor, *What Lesbians Do*, 1975.

Contributor, *Visible, Combining Our Own, a Web of Crones,* and *Women: A Journal of Liberation,* Vol 4, No. 4, "Aging" issue. (song in both, "We Are Like Trees") 1976.

Art Exhibit, "the way we are: ruth mountaingrove's photographs" …60 photographs of The New Woman as she makes her own culture in the Women's Movement. Gertrude's Silver Eighth Note Cafe, Eugene, Oregon, Dec. 1975 - Jan.1976.

Book/Long Poem, *For Those Who Cannot Sleep*, New Woman Press, Grants Pass, OR 1977.

Coordinator & Photographer at "The Ovular", Annual summer workshops for lesbian feminist photographers on women's land, Rootworks, Oregon, 1979-1983.

Artist Contributor, *Azalea*, a magazine by and for third world lesbians, Vol. 4, no. 1, Winter 1980-1981.

Contributor, *a woman's touch*, vol. 1, no. VIII. Aug. 1982.

Editor, Commentator, Essayist and Photographic Contributor, *The Blatant Image*. Includes "The Ovular" photographers. No. 1 1981, No. 2 1982, No. 3 1983.

Contributor, Historian, *Lesbian Land*, by Joyce Cheney, Word Weavers, Minneapolis, MN. Rootworks article by Ruth & Jean Mountaingrove. 1985.

Art Exhibit, "Ruth Mountaingrove, Feminist Photographer", University of Oregon, Eugene, OR. 1988.

Contributor, *The Beltane Papers, a Journal of Women's Mysteries*, Issue 20, "The WomanSpirit Story" article. Winter's Midst Yule, 9999.

Art Exhibit, "Drawing with Light" The Ink People, Eureka, California. Jan. 1991.

Art Exhibit, juried group show, "West Coast Works of/on Paper", The Ink People, Eureka, CA. ("Regeneration", acrylic on paper, 40"x26") 1991.

Art Exhibit, Selected work from the visual arts program of CSU Summer Arts ("Flute Player", digital inkjet print 10"x8") 1992.

Contributor, *Alternative Visions*, University of California, San Diego Women's Journal 1993.

Contributor, *Common Lives/Lesbian Lives* Quarterly #53, Winter, 1995.

Talk Show Host, "Through the Eyes of Women", Women's Radio Collective, KHSU 1990s.

Columnist for the *Senior News*, "The Electronic Highway", Arcata, California in the 1990s.

Book Reviewer and Contributor for the *L-Word* newsletter, Bayside, California, 1991- 2015.

Contributor, *Sinister Wisdom*, No. 64, No. 70, No. 77, No. 84, Berkeley, California, 2005-2011.

Poetry chapbook, *I Remind Myself*, The L-Word Publishers, Bayside, California. 2015.

Art Exhibit, "River of Time, the Remarkable Ruth Mountaingrove", Ink People Center for the Arts. Collected works. 2018.

Art Exhibit, Group Show, "Notable Women of Humboldt County" 2020, Clarke Historical Museum, Eureka, California.

Not mentioned in the above: Exhibitions in: California, Massachusetts, Oregon, Pennsylvania, Texas, and Washington. Contributor to: *The Hamburg Item*, 1939-1940; *Keystone*, 1941-1945; *Woman's Day*, 1948; *Venture*, 1949 (editor, publisher); *Baby Care*, 1950; Columnist, various articles (Bucks County, PA) 1951-1960.

A number of the poems in this book were included in Ruth's 2015 book, *I Remind Myself*. "For Those Who Cannot Sleep" was included in *Country Women*, *Ain't I a Woman*, and the *Eugene Women's Press*. The poem, "For my Muse" was published in *Manzanita Quarterly*, and the poem "Black Silk" was published in *Sinister Wisdom*.

Black Silk and Other Poems, Creative Work of Ruth Mountaingrove

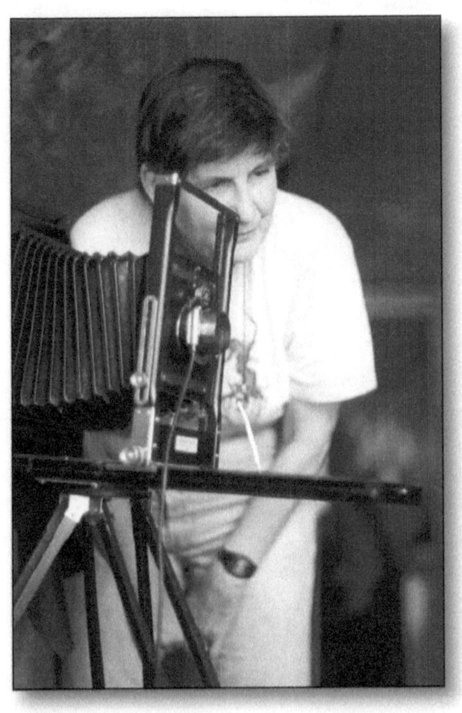

Many Names Press
Blue Lake, California

First Edition.
ISBN 978-1-944497-10-1
Library of Congress Control Number: 2025934008

Kate Hitt, ManyNamesPress.com
Email: khitt@manynamespress.com
P.O. Box 737, Blue Lake, CA 95525 USA

Credits
Book & Cover design & formatting: Kate Hitt, Many Names Press.
Cover: *Drawing with Light #697s*, Ruth Mountaingrove, *Ruth & Pat McCutcheon at Northtown Books 2015*, photos © Cheryle Easter.
Portrait of Ruth, Sketch © PGar (Pat Gargaetas).
Audre Lorde quote from *The Blatant Image No. 1*, 1981.
Ruth in the Darkroom Printing Drawings with Light, photo © Cheryle Easter.
Portrait of Ruth with 4x5 format camera © PGar (Pat Gargaetas).
Women Reading the Blatant Image on the Rootworks Backhoe, 1983, Ruth Mountaingrove, University of Oregon Special Collections.
WomanSpirit #1 Cover, University of Oregon Special Collections.
Ruth and Grandson, Estate of Ruth Mountaingrove.
Suzanne and Ruth on her couch © Suzanne Snider.
Group shot at Ovular #5 © Kate Hitt.
Drawing with Light #741s by Ruth Mountaingrove, photo © Cheryle Easter.
Drawing with Light #038 by Ruth Mountaingrove, photo © Cheryle Easter.
Drawing with Light Images (with Ruth in bed)#756, photo © Cheryle Easter.
Käthe Kollwitz Self Portrait 1934 crayon & brush lithograph, Public Domain.
Self Portrait © Ruth Mountaingrove, University of Oregon Special Collections.
Drawing with Light #9908 by Ruth Mountaingrove, photo © Cheryle Easter.
Drawing with Light #9909 by Ruth Mountaingrove, photo © Cheryle Easter.
Vinnie and Ruth © Debbi Krukonis.
Sue Hilton with Ruth Mountaingrove Self Portrait © Cheryle Easter.
Kate Hitt, Ovular 1983 © Janice Baker.

DEDICATION

for Nancy Ryan,
Ruth's long-time close friend and sister poet
who has shared Ruth's poems with all of us.

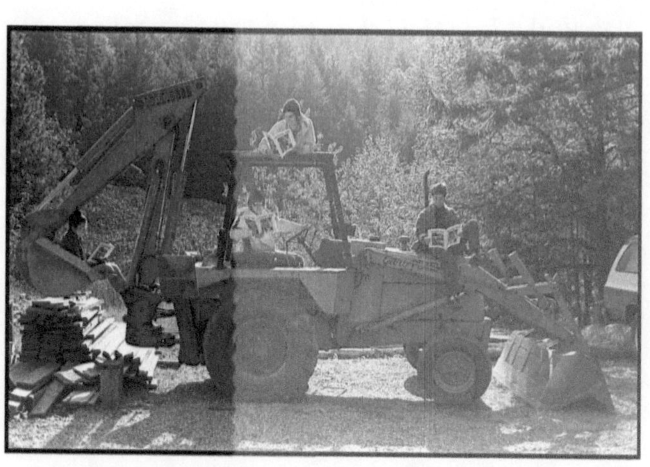

ACKNOWLEDGMENTS

Deep appreciation to the poet Nancy Ryan, who Ruth entrusted with her poetry, and Ruth's daughter, Heather Ikeler, who gave us permission to reproduce Ruth's work.

Thank you, Ink People of Eureka, California, for the Organizational Capacity & Innovation Grant Sue Hilton and *The L-Word* nonprofit acquired to make this book.

Thanks to the University of Oregon Special Collections & University Archives (SCUA). Many of the writings and images used here were in their repository of 74 boxes (*Ruth Mountaingrove Papers, Collection Identifier: Coll 309*). Thank you Kate Hitt, who not only formatted, edited and published the book at Many Names Press, after acquiring the original selection of poems from Vinnie Peloso and Sue Hilton, but also drove to the University of Oregon archives to select more of Ruth's poetry and photographs.

Thanks also to the keepers of Ruth's art, images and photos: Cheryle Easter, Karrie Wallace & Juli Palmer. Thank you to Bonnie MacGregor for her biography, and Suzanne Snider for her remembrance. Thank you to Janice Baker and Pat Gargaetas (PGar) for their photographs.

Thank you, Dan Zev Levinson and Pat McCutcheon, for lending your poetry editing skills and important feedback on the organization, tone and format of the poems. Thanks to A. E. Schulz who edited the final copy with Kate.

In addition, thank you to all those who chose poems initially: Wallace Anderson, Michael Bickford, Susan Dambroff, Jeff DeMark, Aline Faben, Chris Kammler, Debra Kearns, Susan Kornfeld, Chris Orr, Cyndy Phillips, Jim Steinberg, Bob Sizoo and Jana Zvibleman.

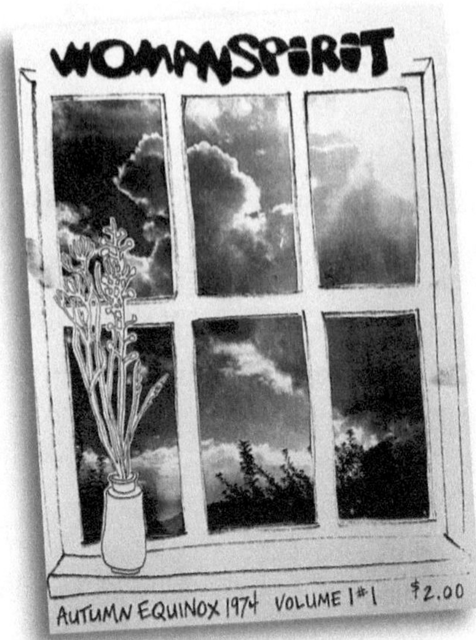

WOMANSPIRIT
AUTUMN EQUINOX 1974   VOLUME 1 #1 $2.00

TABLE OF CONTENTS

Part One, The Lyrical

Part Two, Love & Community

Part Three, Time & Aging

Part Four

Disjunctive Poem in 72 Parts, page 153

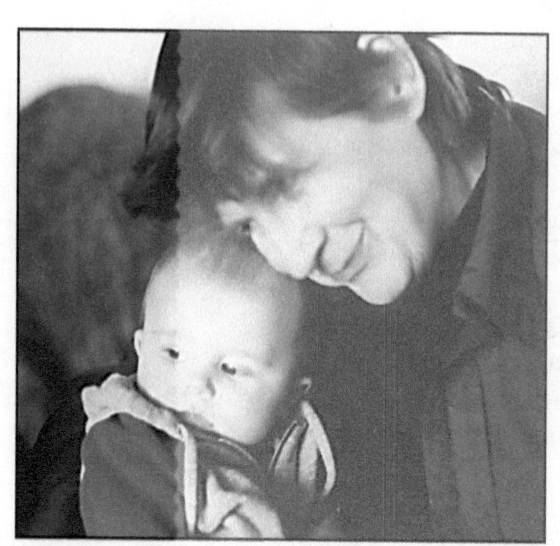

Ruth Mountaingrove (1923-2016) by Bonnie MacGregor

Ruth's story could not be told without her archives, her publications and the memories of her friends. But to fully appreciate how remarkable a woman she was, it is also important to understand her in the context of the times in which she lived.

Ruth was born in 1923 in Philadelphia to working class Pennsylvania Dutch parents. She was their only child and grew up in small towns in Pennsylvania. She was thrown on her own in several ways when she was a young girl: during a year-long separation from her parents because of her mother's illness when she was 4; and, during what she described as the crushing years of the Great Depression that dragged on for most of her childhood. Out of this early—perhaps forced—independence she discovered some of her life-long interests. She received a chemistry set and bought her first camera while she was in junior high school. She learned to rely on her own intuition, intelligence, and determination. These core strengths would be with her throughout the life she later described as "a journey with no map and no path."

Due to her determination to not live such a hard working class existence, Ruth did piecework in a textile factory to save for the fifty dollar tuition to go to Kutztown State Teachers College. She was happy to support herself working in both the chemistry and photography labs, and as the business manager and photo editor of the college yearbook. This was an exciting time to be a young woman and in college, while World War II was taking place. Women were discovering both their own potential and that of other women as they worked in jobs usually reserved for men. There was much talk of a European bohemian lifestyle, and as Ruth discovered poetry and her ability as a writer, she imagined going to Paris and living on the West Bank after the war. Life seemed so open and exciting.

Ruth graduated in 1945, the year the war ended, and immediately got a job teaching science. She got her own apartment and made enough money to publish her first book of poetry, *Rhythms of Spring*. While waiting to be recognized as a poet she met a young school teacher, Bern Ikeler, and they married in 1946.

The expansive future abruptly changed when men came back from the war and that self-fulfilling time for women ended. The romantic movies and magazines that had extolled the strengths of women now projected an idealized image of a happy family life and entreated the women to go back home and fulfill their true roles as housewives and mothers.

Ruth stopped working and took on the life of a suburban housewife and mother in the 1950s, but continued writing even as she gave birth to her four boys: Eric (who died of pneumonia,) Kim, Jeff and David. Ruth intended to maintain her dream of self-fulfillment, but it was hard to integrate her life with being a poet. As she wrote during those years: "I lose myself to find my way...."

Life in the 1950s, for a great many women, including Ruth, who had tasted that independence in the war years, was very conflicted. They both embraced aspects of their roles as wives and mothers and chafed at the losses to themselves of their very sense of self. That chafing often led to conflict with their husbands who struggled to uphold what society said was man's rightful dominance. Most all of this conflict happened behind closed doors, and as part of the family dynamics the children grew up in. It was rough on Ruth's children at times and she knew it.

Ruth wrote about what those years were like for her emotionally in a long poem she later published, with an informative introduction, titled *For Those Who Cannot Sleep*. She refers to this time as "this dark time-chilled country" where "the stranger in my heart betrays my never-known."

Just as the 1960s burst forth with the Civil Rights and Peace and Student Movements, and women began to wake up, Ruth was made pregnant again. Her daughter Heather was born in 1961. The oppressive feeling of having another small child to care for just as her boys were becoming more independent led to more clashes with Bern. Ruth went into Jungian analysis to try to cope, but it made her realize she needed to end the marriage. And so, as her son recalled: "she booted him out and changed the locks." It was 1963 and Ruth was 40 years old.

For the next six years Ruth raised her four children, ranging in age from two to fourteen, by herself while working full time as a chemical technician. She discovered Betty Friedan's *The Feminine Mystique* and realized she was not alone at all. Many people credit the book with sparking the beginning of the second wave of feminism in this country. The book came out in 1963, so Ruth was on board pretty much from the beginning. She searched out the local National Organization for Women (NOW) chapter, went to talks and workshops, and met lots of women sharing her conundrums and experiences.

It was in a single parent workshop sponsored by NOW that she met Jean, who would be the impetus for Ruth to become who she truly wanted to be.

Ruth called her transition "breaking through into my own life," from East Coast suburban housewife and lonely poet Ruth Ikeler to West Coast lesbian-separatist cultural innovator Ruth Mountaingrove. It took several years. The divorce went through in 1965, and she won a custody battle for her daughter. She sold all she could, and then headed West in 1971 with ten-year-old Heather and nineteen-year-old Jeff to join Jean and her two children at Mountain Grove Commune. Ruth was 48 years old.

This journey was both trans-continental and transformational. It was the liberation part of what we called then the "Women's Liberation Movement". Ruth later wrote in the afterword of *For Those Who Cannot Sleep:*

> *I live close to my unconscious. I am a slumberer and I need to wake up, to become conscious. My intuition works very well for me. I do not like to work out all the steps between my insight and my understanding. But integration holds riches for me. I cannot sleep.*

> *I am being offered a second chance for and inner and outer change in which I can become a whole person, 'a woman and man, and more and more,' I wrote in a song-prayer three years ago. A chance to go on journeys deep into my psyche. A chance to journey over and over. This is a great gift of life.*

Ruth and Jean Mountaingrove lived together at three different rural communes in Oregon: Mountain Grove, Cabbage Lane, and Golden before they bought their own "women's land" called Rootworks, in 1978. Ruth's creativity blossomed. Some of her poetry became songs and inspired song circles. Fed by the freedom from societal expectations, surrounded by meadows and forests that healed her, Ruth was able to explore love with no defined script, and with a woman who was generous, smart and supportive and whose skills complimented hers.

Not only did they learn to fix their cars and saw up downed trees to provide their heat, along with other women they built barns and planted the gardens that provided their food. They were now "Country Women"—raising children who needed to get to school through the snow on dirt roads that had not been plowed. Everything they needed required them to learn to provide for themselves...and they did...with a lot of help from their women friends, working collectively.

As women over fifty, Ruth and Jean brought to the land many abilities and valuable expertise. Together they not only secured the physical haven of Rootworks as land trust and as Women's Land in perpetuity, they created three significant cultural vehicles that provided a generation of women the way to find our own voices, define our own culture, and live into our own images. Those vehicles were *WomanSpirit* magazine; *The Blatant Image*, a magazine of feminist photography; and the songbook, *Turned On Women*.

A dissertation, if not a book, could and should be written about the influence of these works on women's lives. *WomanSpirit* printed the poetry, songs, photographs, drawings, articles and rituals of hundreds of women from across the country—known and unknown—for ten years, from 1974 to 1984.

The magazine inspired and influenced thousands of women searching for a new way to be. I was one of them. All of these efforts were accomplished as Ruth and Jean drew to themselves groups of women who learned from each other and with each other how to do what they needed to live off the land, collectively.

This era of the 1970s and early 1980s and their rural-inspired, innovative ventures were part of a web of uniquely women-identified ventures in cities and towns across the country and around the world. And, although that culture has become fragmented in recent decades, the spirit of inclusive, collective, creative self-determination of women permeates our lives and some institutions to this day.

Ruth and Jean lived together for 12 years. When their relationship ended it was not just a painful personal loss, it meant that Ruth also lost her home and community. She left Rootworks and began searching for another relationship and place to be.

She heard that California colleges offered advanced degree programs to people over 60 and this inspired her. On a visit to Arcata at the invitation of Belle Shalom, she took a look at Humboldt State University and decided to move here in 1986. Although she was often lonely, or perhaps *because* she was, she called upon her creative determination to jump into new endeavors. She enrolled in the Master in Fine Arts program and started working with Belle and Ina Harris producing the a new radio show on KHSU, "Through the Eyes of Women", interviews by, for, and about women, that aired until 2019, when Humboldt State eliminated all community-run programs. She earned her first MFA in 1990 at 67.

Throughout the 1990s, Ruth found more ways to be in community and work collaboratively with women. She joined the board of directors of Humboldt Women for Shelter and took charge of the darkroom at The Ink People, exploring and teaching photographic techniques, as she continued to produce and mentor women with "Through the Eyes of Women."

Ruth wrote articles and poems for publication, and hung her artwork in galleries as far away as Florida. She also found *us*, a small but talented lesbian community, with whom she could develop close friendships and sing her songs at the Lesbohemian Coffeehouse. She wrote book reviews for the *L-Word* newsletter, and joined a small group of poets in a writers' group.

As Ruth entered her seventies, she embraced her elder-hood with creativity. She bought a computer, and with her love of technical exploration and teaching, she not only learned to use it but also proofread and wrote a column for the *Senior News* monthly newspaper on the subject of all the computer's possibilities. She was an editor of the Older

Lesbians Organizing for Change newsletter for three years. She enjoyed a couple of lovers and learned to savor the benefits of living alone independently.

From 1988-1997, Ruth produced a videotaped autobiography with 21 videotapes of her life and work which is now in the University of Oregon Special Collections, which houses a very large feminist archive. She capped off her seventies with a Masters in Theater Arts degree from Humboldt State University after writing and producing a play called *Hats* at 79.

In 2015, at the age of 92, her chapbook *I Remind Myself* was produced by The L-Word publishers, and she gave her last public reading. She continued writing her book reviews for the *L-Word* and attending her writers' group until she just couldn't anymore due to her health. The circles of women became increasingly smaller but they still sustained and inspired her. That mutuality of interest and affection even extended to the young people who started coming to help her out: students from Y.E.S. (Youth Educational Services). at Humboldt State, willing and able younger lesbians and friends, and finally the Visiting Angels and Hospice caregivers with the P.A.C.E. program.

One of the hardest chapters of this magnum opus that was her life was the letting go at the end: letting go of her forward momentum, her autonomy, and so many of her abilities. But even in this, she was never alone. All the inspiration, innovation, and guidance she had given to others drew to her a group of capable, constant and caring friends who, usually at Ruth's direction, orchestrated making sure she was taken care of in the ways she wanted to be to the very end. In this, she also taught us, through them, how to do that for each other in the years to come.

Ruth died on December 18, 2016. She was 93 years old.

Bonnie MacGregor,
Arcata, California

Ruth Mountaingrove, a Remembrance by Suzanne Snider

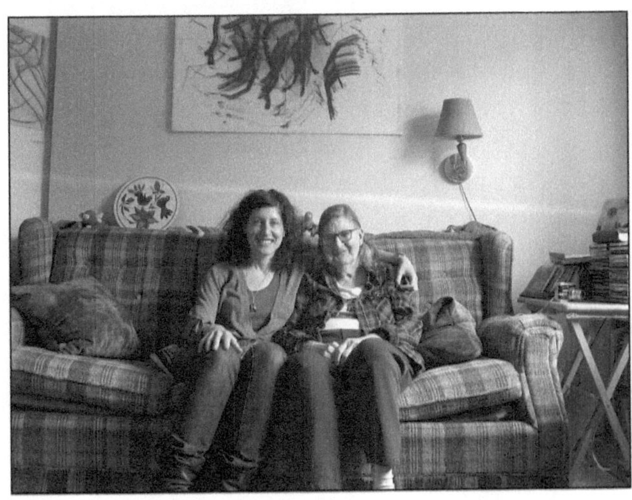

I probably knew Ruth the least of everyone gathered together, but I take pride in being a recent friend; my good fortune.

In 2011, I traveled along part of the West Coast to record oral histories with women who ran radical presses and print shops between 1960 and 1985, often overlapping with the project of documenting the lesbian separatist movement as it existed in the 1970s, and 1980s.

Though Ruth's story did not resemble my own life experience (I'm 44 years old), I embraced it as part of my originology and my future. So many interviewees spent our interview time reminiscing and looking back, which I supported, but oral history is also an invitation to look at the present moment and to look ahead to the future, and this is an invitation that Ruth heartily embraced. Our interview seamlessly turned into a studio visit where I had the chance to look at her recent work and discuss the questions she wanted to explore in 2011 through photography—and later, into a quasi-book group, discussing recent books that came out by our favorite lesbian authors.

As it happens, our recording session was pitted against "edging day," the one day a month that someone cleaned up the grass outside her home. We paused the recorder repeatedly. On the upside, Ruth often wrote to me on subsequent "edging days," because it reminded her of our interview and time together. When my daughter was born, Ruth asked to see photographs and inquired about her and about my writing projects.

I took many photographs of interviewees I met during this oral history trip in 2011, but I think that Ruth is the only person from whom I sought permission to photograph us together, as well. I treasure this picture of us side by side. I remember a true feeling of kinship with my arm around her and hers around me.

Cumulatively, her photographs told me a real story as well, of growth and change—of successfully moving beyond nostalgia and continually changing the way we look at our world and subverting the way our world looks at us.

I'm honored to have spent time with Ruth, and to have recorded some of her life history.

Suzanne Snider,
New York

Channeling Ruth
at Many Names Press, 2025

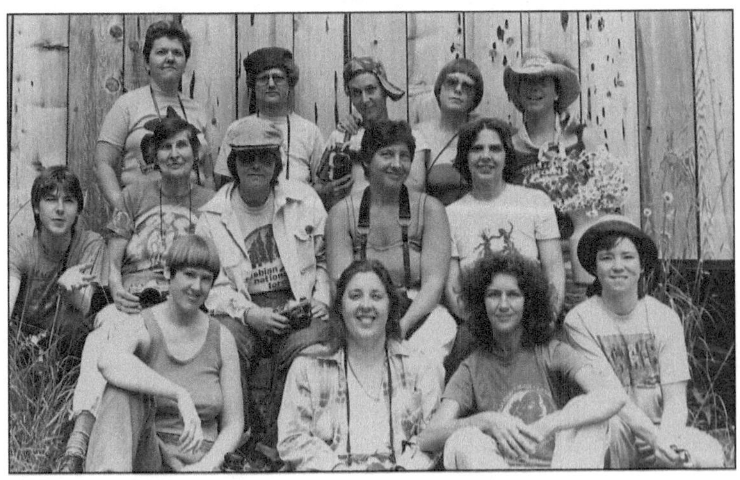

Me (bottom right) & My Ovular Friends 1983

Almost four decades ago, shortly after she had moved to Arcata, Ruth Mountaingrove, an accomplished photographer and writer, handed me her manuscript—a feminist play in the form of a Greek classic, with a little Lillian Hellman thrown in. She wanted me to publish it even then.

When I lived in Humboldt in the early 1980s, there were several rural women's communities in Southeastern Oregon where lesbians were free to just "be", and the Mountaingrove's property Rootworks was the most creative and liberating of them all.

I first met Ruth and Jean at the Ovular #5 workshop in 1983, and then wrote about it for *The Blatant Image* (No. 3). I was an offset press operator, with a working knowledge of pre-digital age photography—an integral part of the printing process, as any printer will tell you. There was no electricity at Rootworks, just solar power. We shared meals outside together, made prints in the solar-powered darkroom, ran around the land, held photo shoots, shows, laughed, cried, and got down with our bad selves. We could wander the creative landscape freely, away from all the societal rules that cried, *privileged straight white men only*. Even the name "Ovular" for the workshop series was perfect: round-sounding and not so patriarchal like "SEMINar". You get the picture if you've ever been a radical separatist, like we were then.

Ruth wanted me to print and publish her play, but at that time I had not become the literary publisher that I am today. So, it feels rather serendipitous that Sue Hilton and Vinnie Peloso (who did an amazing job of compiling most of the poems first) asked me to produce and publish this first edition of Ruth's selected work.

Sue acquired the funding I requested through the *L-Word* newsletter nonprofit and The Ink People. I drove to Eugene and the University of Oregon archives to sift through some of the 74 boxes of Ruth's writing and photographs, using my smartphone to take pictures of each item—both text and image, which speeded things up immensely. When I got home, I incorporated some into the book, and added a few of my own photos from the Ovular #5.

Ruth was in the hurricane's eye of an age when social attitudes toward lesbians and aging women were shifting for the better. She fought hard for her right to be independent and retain her jobs, for her degree while solely supporting her children; she became a lesbian deep in love, in a serious and long relationship until they broke it off. Everything Ruth went through in the end helped her grow creatively, and have freedom to think and feel deeply, to follow truth, to be treated equally, to be loving and kind yet fierce, to develop respect and dignity for women and one's self— to me, she was a brave and beautiful feminist living the artist's life.

It is my hope that this book will provide us all courage and inspiration to keep resisting the white masculinist patriarchy that is ripping away our freedom and rights (to our bodies, equality, privacy, finances, homes, etc.) as I write this.

Kate Hitt, Blue Lake, California

Foreword

I first met Ruth Mountaingrove in the summer of 1993. That year, I attended the Port Townsend Writers' Conference where the poet Linda Gregg encouraged me to start a poetry group at home, adding that the best groups didn't necessarily consist of good poets, but good readers of poetry, people willing and able to offer useful feedback about what was on the page.

Upon returning to Arcata, California, I stood up at the next open mike at the Jambalaya Club and asked if anyone present wanted to form a poetry group. Ruth was the first to say yes. And from that time until shortly before she died in 2016, Ruth and I would meet every two or three weeks to workshop each other's verse. Over the years, others moved in and out of our group. In 1994, Pat McCutcheon, another local poet, joined us. For years, it was just us three writing, reading, critiquing and growing as poets, readers and friends.

I'm sure many of Ruth's women friends were baffled by our relationship. After all, by the time I met her, Ruth was a well-known West Coast radical lesbian separatist. At first, I was baffled myself.

I soon learned, however, that she and I had both grown up on the East Coast. We were both only children. And I am about the same age as her son David would have been had he not taken his own life in his twenties—the "sensitive, poetic one," Ruth would say. Ruth was also about the same age as my mother, at the time living three thousand miles away. Together, Ruth and I shared our memories, stories, jokes and poems. Ruth had a wicked sense of humor. Frankly, I was flattered, but a little intimidated.

When Ruth died in 2016, her extensive recordings, photography, workshops, magazines, journals and fine art (including her exhibitions and radio shows) went to the

University of Oregon where they are currently archived at the Knight Library. But her poetry, left by Ruth to her friend Nancy Ryan, remained with the *L-Word* newsletter editor Sue Hilton in Arcata, California. Nancy's vision loss prevented her from sorting and editing Ruth's poems, so Sue asked me if I would be interested. That was over six years ago. This volume is the result of our efforts.

In addition to the three self-published volumes Ruth put together in her lifetime: *Rhythms of Spring, For Those Who Cannot Sleep* and *I Remind Myself*, Sue had hundreds more poems Ruth wrote in various stages of completion. Some were assignments for the creative writing classes Ruth took—most notably with Judith Minty at Humboldt State University (now Cal Poly Humboldt) in the 1980s. Many more were written for our poetry group that met regularly in our homes.

Even though Ruth was receptive to criticism, she was firm in her own ideas. Skimming through these poems for the collection, I found that Ruth didn't revise much. I don't think you could say she followed Ginsberg's "first thought, best thought" mantra, but there is little evidence that she reworked her poems. Most of Ruth's poems were free verse, although some were in the traditional forms of pantoums, sestinas, ballads and sonnets. Overall, I think you can safely say most were composed in the moment: fresh, hot and raw.

If, as I believe, feminism was the defining literary movement of my generation, opening the door for gay and lesbian literature, ethnic studies, multiculturalism and spoken word, then Ruth Mountaingrove was my Virgil, guiding me first in and down, then up and out into our currently diverse and pluralistic poetic universe.

Reading through her poems, one is struck by the prevalence of a soft or "feminine" line ending for many of them. While this may help give the poems a "suggestion of colloquial informality, or lightness…" (*The Princeton Encyclopedia of Poetry and Poetics,)* I like to think Ruth was also consciously striking a blow against the "prosodic patriarchy" through her lineation.

Ruth always had clear values and goals in addition to her sense of humor. Upon coming into some money in the mid-nineties, she debated whether to use this windfall for a new set of teeth or a new computer. Of course, she chose the computer.

In 2015, at the age of ninety-two, Ruth gave her last public reading. She died on December 18, 2016 at the age of ninety-three. She was writing into the last weeks of her life.

Vincent Peloso,
Fortuna, California

Part One

The Lyrical

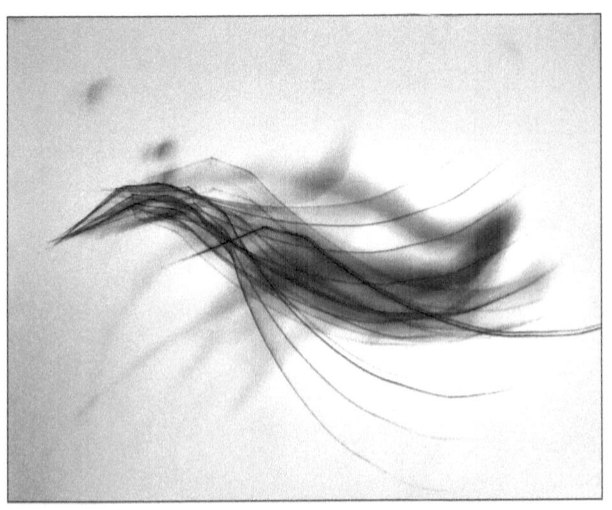

A Doppler View

Fog
A doppler view.
Receding.

The trees of many unmatched greens.
Needles of rain.
A wave of mailboxes,
Yellow, gray, white.

Cold, numbed feet,
Stiff hands.

Horses
Viewed through a cleared space;
Standing stoically.

The heavy sound of stitching rain,
Needle rain
On the car's cloth top
Over my head,
Obscuring my windshield,
Making my seeing translucent.

I think of you
Who will read this poem
In some hot dry summer,
Will feel the bone chill
Of the day,
Will hear the stitching rain,
Will look translucently
Through my rainfilled windshield
At horses standing stoically....

I have settled for less in a poem.

Age

A white withered magpie
with living eyes
sitting in a nest
of dusty wallpaper,
dropped from the ceiling
in time's exhaustion,
remembers Lincoln.
She sat on his lap,
or was that Whitman?

And just the other day
Emerson was saying…
Or was it Thoreau?
Now where was she?
Hobbling through tunnels
of cobwebbed books
balancing like Pisa;
living in a time
that marries all time.

The magpie's eyes
are fires in the gloom
of this house
where the porch boards
are rotten
and the steps
have crumbled away.
A thin electric light
hangs from the ceiling.

(A very old poem, written as Ruth Ikeler, in Lambertville, NJ.)

Amrak

after small rains
whiffs of dust
for the sage is heavy with ash
and smoke leavens in the ovens
of memory.   tanic, tart, it wakes
me and I hold in the hand that is not
reaching for a crutch the words Los Alamos
staining my palms, bruising my fingers.
the bomb grew hand by hand when I was young
and now I am old and here
with the tinder of neglect, the dry mouth of fear
becoming crowns and spot fires
that run swiftly as water did once.
the fire line the work of good intentions
unclear whether the thinning
was nature's stewardship or smudged hard hats.
the canyons are streamers that cut the throat
remembering yet another fall from grace.
we are replicators who with ease rise
only to ruin, rather than understand
what remains from fire to fire,
as the ice melts.

Ancestors

In a riverbank grove
wind nudges treetops,
then whips up a limb swaying brouhaha.
A gust flips through my notebook,
poem after poem rapidly rise, salute and fall.
How long ago were my pages living trees?
How long ago the inescapable sacrifice?
I want to write
what is in the pages
before they became pages.

Appreciating a Turquoise Bowl

Go to it

new
    alive
        vibrant
with living.

Gaze
    deep
and dredge
from memory's floor
        cerulean skies
      tumultuous ocean
         and
         the vivid heart
           of
                a flower.

Let the eye
      round
        in the bowl's circle
and remember
      limitless horizons
on the sand edge
      skies at dawn
        half
           circle of stars
        half
           dawn light
and
    the round line
        of the moon.

Different Songs

When spring has come and winter's gone
then summer wants to have her turn.
The flowers bloom across the marsh
and birds sing many different songs.

You walk with me beside these flowers,
a tapestry of many colors.
The gulls fly by, the bees engage
in making honey for their hive.

You walk with me around this pond.
We talk of life and what's to come.
You hold each hour a precious jewel;
you live each day as though your last.

I walk with you along this path.
A path I've walked a long time before
when I reached out for sorrow's hand
and held it clasped within my own.

And I would wish you happiness
and I would wish you joy indeed.
and I would wish you courage, strength
to meet the days you are moving through.

When flowers bloom across the marsh
and birds sing many different songs,
when spring has come and winter's gone,
then summer wants to have her turn.

Eurydice and Orpheus Update
Six Monologues

1. Eurydice

Men! When I was alive
he was too busy.
He had to make it while he
could, he'd say.
Sweet smell of success.
While I sat home alone
he's traipsing all over the country
totally into his work,
playing his Martin,
singing his songs,
seducing the women....

Now when I finally
have some peace. When
I no longer care,
he comes crying for me
to come back. He misses
me. Writes me songs like
Tom Paxton's song of regret:
It's a lesson too late for the learning…
Swears he'll charm Death
with his singing and playing.
Well he doesn't charm me.
I've had it with this boy
and his singing.

2. Groupie in the Park

Hey! Listen, she didn't
know what she had. That
voice. Oh, God! that voice.

I could have died for that
voice. And he was so beautiful.
Listen, when he sang
it was like what can I tell
you   the birds stopped
singing. No kidding
I was there, and listen
it really happened.
And not only that but
there was this rabbit—
just went and sat at his feet.

He was always phoning her
even when he was doing
all those concerts.
He never saw me at all.

3. Butch, Eurydice's Lesbian Lover

No, I don't believe it.
She never killed herself.
She loved life. She
loved me. Oh, I knew
how she felt about him.
But he wasn't worth
this. What will I do
without her? She…
so beautiful. Her skin
silk under my hands
lips opening to
mine   my tongue…
What proof is
there? Who told you?
We were going to live
together after she left
him. I wanted to.
She wasn't so sure.

Said she was getting
too old for marriage.
Besides I am a woman.

4. Ed, Gay Lover of Orpheus

Yeah. I know him.
He likes rough trade.
I give him what he
asks for. His songs
are for me. She
never knew about
us. I met him at a
rest stop. He was
sitting on a table
playing his guitar
and singing.
                    I
asked if I could
travel with him.
I was just bumming
around. He always
was the woman with
me. I don't know
what he was with her.
And I don't want to know.
He loves me
That's all I care about.

5. Persephone, Queen of the Underworld

Just who does he think
he is? Coming down here
acting as though he owned
this place. Him and his
guitar. Why didn't he
love her when he had her?

These poets. Think they
can sing their way out of
anything. And she doesn't
want to go back. That's
clear.
      But what a seducer
he is. Even the boat woman
who should have known better.
She's supposed to stop her
ears when these poets sing.

6. Orpheus

Alright. I wasn't the best
husband. I didn't love her.
That's always the way it is
with makers. She never could
get that. Thought I should
stay home more. I needed
applause. Those admiring
eyes.
      Now I would go
through hell to have her.
She gave me my songs.
What will I do without her
in my bed. How will I stay
warm? She made me a god.

What is left but to go
get her. Bring her back.
But here's a catch.
I don't doubt my power to
sing. But what if she
doesn't want to   she
doesn't want to come back.

For My Muse

"Write me a poem," she said
curling my hair around her finger,
distracting my mind into feeling.
"Write of how you love me,"
she said, touching my ear,
making me lose my words
down corridors of desire.
"Make me a poem of fire."

I, helpless, reached for a verb
to build passion bit by bit,
for nouns to layer my heart,
while she traced a bracelet
around my wrist, laughing.
Making a poem of fire.

Forgotten Head, 1967

Well now I've got to run she said,
Went out the door, forgot her head.
The eyebrows lifted with dismay,
Come back mouth said, don't go that way,
You are not thinking what you've done,
Just because you've got to run.
Come back, put on your hat, your hair
But she kept going down the stair.

Outside nobody seemed to know,
They didn't look or see her go
Blindly through that dreaming town
Dressed in her Givenchy gown,
Stiletto heels, crazy hose,
Without her ears, without her nose.

Freesia

When the white
freesia
have stopped
blooming
it will be time
to turn on
the heat.

Summer
caught in these white
flowers
will fall
into
Fall
like these freesia
dropping petal
by petal
off green stems
held in the round
pink
pottery
vase.

When the freesia
stop
blooming
fall
I can
have warm
mornings.
Get up
from my bed
into
Summer.

Full Moon Night

The moon
slipped
over my
windowsill
and
broke
on my
pillow
scattering
pieces
in my
eye.

Harmonica

The haunting
sounds
of the
harmonica

swirl
through
the ear
stirs
memory

My first
instrument
two keys
C on the top
G on the bottom

Lost now
many
years
many
moves
many
lives

Companion
in lonely
nights
played softly

A harmonica
in G
I play
tonight.

I Carry Patches of Sunlight In My Pockets

I carry patches of sunlight in my pocket
so poems raise the veins on my wrists.
They begin in my ears, a deaf dance
speak out loud for my bleary eyes
move birds in the branches like wind.
Walking backwards into sound are
shadows, maps of being on the way,
rolled and folded up.
Blue lines, water where
poems float without touching bottom
while stones slip with their carrying song
catch in the calms. Cross twigs
stir doldrums with rain.
Over land, under stories check
too much ease and sap glues
the dream book bounded smooth.
Young poems happen easily
like lips, tongue, teeth playing
at syllables without looking back
from their three legged play
their urgency, thrust deep
beaver biting, pushing a knowing
a shelter, as yet unknown
for going under when age comes.

Letters to Wang Lei

I

When Wang Lei left by the North Gate
she said she would write
before the ice stones thawed in the river.

The snow has melted into forsythia.
Along the banks ducks swim lazily.
No letter comes to the North Gate
where Chu-sing goes daily
to stare at the empty mountains.

How lonely it is without you, Chu-sing cries.
My heart is a blinded bird.

II

Cold winds still pour from the mountains
whirling the pink blossoms in the garden.
Yesterday the grass bent with the rain.

You left me your quilted red kimono
and your ivory fan.

There are ice flowers on the river.

My heart begins to see again
dimly with double vision.

And if you came back again, Wang Lei?

Painting Outdoors

The shadows of the fence
fall on leveled weed
the stream is a mud
ditch fed by empty
culverts. Birds still
sing above the passing
traffic but there are no
stalks to rest upon
no grasses.
      The
blackberries are long
gone though a mosquito
birthed by the sun
considers dinner
a black spider runs up
my knee.

I trespass on this scene
casting a shadow like
this fence. Inspectors
inspect me
challenge my right
to winter sun. A spider web
gleams.
      Frame this with
silence intermittent.
Hang it on your mind's
wall.

Rent to a Poet

Poets are much less messy.

True, they do leave unfinished lines,
even stanzas about the place.
Cleaning, you find a forgotten
poem under the couch pillow.
Filling up wastebaskets you forget
to empty them. They leave the
typewriter on the kitchen table
and wander off, mumbling.

    But
that is nothing. The real messy
renters are artists. Pastels, oils,
watercolors, tempera, charcoal
all over the walls and floor. Some
hurling paint, walking in it
with their shoes or bare feet.

Poets only need a small notebook.
A pen that works. In an emergency
a pencil will do.

    The artist will
scatter clay on your floor, carve marks
in your kitchen table, hot glue the
formica. S/he will line the walls
with canvases, done or undone;
fill the air with turpentine and
linseed oil.

Rent to a poet

any time.

Sand Dollars

Lovers and friends
have brought me sand dollars.
Sand dollars rest on my table
on my window sill
drizzling sand
from various beaches
Mad River, Trinidad
Clam. These are perfect
sand dollars.

The ones I find
are attacked by gulls
ravenous to reach
the interior prize. The
sand dollar cannot
protect itself, its insides
being apparently delicious.

An artist at engraving
each sand dollar's shell
etched with delicate lines
ellipses, circles, symmetrical.
This fragile artist builds
a round protective house,
as artists build round protective shells
that do not protect them either.

The sand dollars blend
with the sand sometimes,
but where do they come from?
These sand dollars. Does
the sea, reaching into their
hiding place, toss them

upon the sand?
Where is their home?
Do they die on land?
Or do the waves come in
tides moving up the beach
take them back?

September Song

—for a Reluctant Lover

With pill and foam and the
Name of a good abortionist
Tucked under your hat band,
What have we to fear? she asked.

Ah, but I really want the child
Said he, to prove again I am a man:
Your child and mine
Would be a genius
Born in a late year to us.

I already have four geniuses, she said.
Children of my heart and soul.
All of my children now will be
Of the spirit, said she:
Poems and songs, painting and dancing.

Sexism, or a Political Poem

Some women will not
shut up. They keep
making the man uncomfortable
by asking questions:
Do you pay your
women workers
what you pay your men?
Have you gone to
bat for a woman for
tenure?
Do you do half
the housework? Which half?

Today on the radio a
man blunders into quicksand,
says to Alice Walker:
The system has done well by you,
and she laughs and laughs
and laughs. *You gotta be kidding,*
she says between guffaws. *The
system done well by me?*

He knows he's sinking, says
lamely, '*The Color Purple*'—
*you must have sold
millions of that book.*
Yes, she says, *and no thanks to
the system,* astounded at his
ignorant arrogance,
she's still laughing
painfully.

The men in my class,

with one exception, do not
understand my poem. Some
would like me to shut up.
Some are struggling.

Listen up: far more men than women
publish poetry, have gallery shows,
make it into the important exhibitions.

Yet women make up
more than half the population
more than half of poetry workshops
more than half of painting classes.

Does that
make it
any
clearer?

Sometimes

Sometimes,
    it's only in the poem
    that we can reach each other
    a phone call
    or even just being together
    is not the same.

We have years to evacuate
    digging down into our many selves.

I can tell you facts
    but what are you feeling?

Where are you?
    And Who?

So we begin…
    Where were you born?
      Yesterday
          before supper
    today before lunch?
          tomorrow?

And how did you grow?
    Crooked bent by trees
      flickering on the water
    Washed by cat's paws
      behind your ears?

See,
    I do not know you.
    We are together
      but not close.

Only in the poem I reach for you
	not to possess you
		but to include you.

Come into my world
	and let me enter yours.

Spider Web

The spider web hangs on the wall.
You brush it down and that is all.
It's gone before your glancing hand,
Just as you planned, just as you planned.

An architecture hung in space,
It brushes lightly on your face,
Then breaks and falls upon the floor
As you walk careless through the door.

The spider hurries to the spot
Incredulous to what is not.
Fragile webs are often broken
By careless hands, by words unspoken.

By white men in another's land.
By strangers when they take command,
Invading towns they do not know
And going where they shouldn't go.

The white man tore the Indian's web
Of buffalo treks with boot heel's tread.
He now determines to destroy
The only earth we can enjoy.

There is a fragile web of life
And we can cut it with a knife,
Destroy that which we cannot see,
Destroy the you, destroy the me.

The spider views the dismal scene,
Remembers where its web has been,
Begins to build again in space

With patience infinite, and grace.

Be careful where your boot heels tread,
Do not destroy the fragile thread.
Invisible community,
The spider web you cannot see.

The Cellar

I remember
that dark cellar,
cold in wintertime
where we
candled the eggs.

We looked for life
and when we found it,
removed it from
the eggs for sale.

We saved those blood
spotted eggs,
the fertile ones
for customers
who ate life whole.

The Light

I remember the light
touching your body -
pink and rose
on that overcast day
as you sat Buddha patient
before my awkward pencil,
my student self
recording lush flesh
in monotones,
before we became
suffused with color,
our hands painting on our bodies
illuminating desire.

Yesterday on a pink background
I re-remembered
painting your body
in rose. Transforming
penciled memory
with the swath of my brush.
Summoning you back
to sit in my studio,
to come alive
under my hand
as I have under yours.

The Promise

He said, destroy them
all my words;
shred them into alphabet
strings;
they die when I die.
Promise.
His friend did.
Followed his orders.
We will never know
what we have lost.

His friend only understood
orders, not disobedience.
Was not curious.
Was not a writer.
Perhaps the words
were garbage
perhaps jewels.
The dead man did not
allow us the judgment.

The friend, keeping his promise
shredded those pages
one by one.
Stories, poems, essays, articles
we will never read.
Lost to us. Not one saved.
Not even a fragment
to honor their creator.
His friend honored him
with oblivion.

Time

The days collapse inside each other
The years condense within the alchemist's retort
Soon it will be dark
Though now the light suns trees and hills
Long days collapse inside long night.
The alchemist understands all
This I do not.

    Why do the years
Swirl of such blackness?
Climbing the walls to condense in drops
Turning nights inside out. What holds the fire
To the days' darkness to burn them into light?

    How can I know living
Inside the cauldron whether it's age
Speeding up my world? Is it this
Fire the alchemist is feeding?
Or are the days really moving faster?
How can I know?

    My instruments
For measuring are useless inside
These walls. Only the alchemist can tell me
And she is feeding my heart
Into the fire watching the blackness
Burn away.

    Are we all in this
Cauldron of transformation spinning
In the swirling vapors? How can we tell
Each other the world moves faster?
How can we tell?

Transformation

Once upon a cat
there was a time.
When she was a kitten
she wore a hat,
when she was a kitten
she was a she
but when she got much bigger
she was a he.

As she, she was cuddled
and snuggled.
As he, he was banned
from the house
mostly because of his
he-ness.

When she was a she
she mothered kittens—
not hers, but she took on
the task. As a he, he
fathered suspicion.
Was he a killer?
Was that the reason
that some kittens died?

When she was a she
she had a girl's name.
Now she is a he;
his name is a boy's.

This transformation
is confusing. Not to he
who has no category

but to us who want to
catalog, separate and group
in neat files.
With this cat-a-list
avert catastrophe.

Two arts once were self taught

Photography
and poetry.
          Now there are
workshops, classes,
degrees
          not for the
good of either
poet or
photographer.
          The
workshop poem.
          The
portfolio photograph.
Something of the soul is
missing.
          There is need to
please
that was not there
before. A narrow band of
critics and critiques.

A coffin to die in? Or a
warning to escape?

Venus

She comes
into our lives
tornadoing
lifting us
up
to set us
down
miles
from where
we have
been.
We slowly
come
to
check our
bones our
lives our
watches
gather up
time
again
smooth out
our maps
check the moss
on trees
find our way
back to who
we are.

Villanelle for Judith

Because there is a level in the mind
a floor with a trap door   I hesitate to raise
down which I seldom go   I pick a rune.

The future is so clear to these old Norse.
Each rune responds   I pick one gingerly.
Because there is a level in the mind

my future is not clear   I walk in fog
wandering my way   choosing a path
down which I seldom go.   I pick a rune.

While it seems strange in this world where I live
there are more worlds and I must deal with them.
Because there is a level in the mind

where shadows live   where words can come alive
a scarey place   a place that stops the heart
down which I seldom go I pick a rune.

thanking   the old wise women where they live
who wish me courage through the stone I hold;
because there is a level in the mind
down which I seldom go   I pick a rune.

Walking Home: A Found Poem

I kick a
silver metal circle off the
road. Rauschenberg would have made
art of that   I think
Bend down
grasp the circle in my
fingers   walk on
Maybe a picture
frame   I think   maybe, or...

I shift the circle from hand to
hand on this chill
morning.
          A block later
Alliance Road strewn with
classical album
sleeves.   Moldy   torn   bent.
I walk on
by.
          Think of Rauschenberg.
His stuffed goat.   His
old rubber tire.   The block
he walked around.
          I stop.
Go back   begin picking up
Chopin, Beethoven, Hummer,
Mozart, Haydn, Handel,
Dvorak.
          Carry the sleeves to my
studio.
          Clean off spider
eggs   fine particles of
dirt.

This morning
I am
Rauschenberg.

Words Fail Me

Sometimes
my unconscious said
there are no
poems.
No poems! said
I. How can that
be?
Always I said.
You never let me
down.
So this is first
said she.
No! No!
I said down on my
knee. Give me a
poem.
Anything
I said. A bird a
dream. The
sea.
She laughed
indulgent stroked my
cheek.
Not this time
dear she said and
walked away from
me.

Part Two

Love & Community

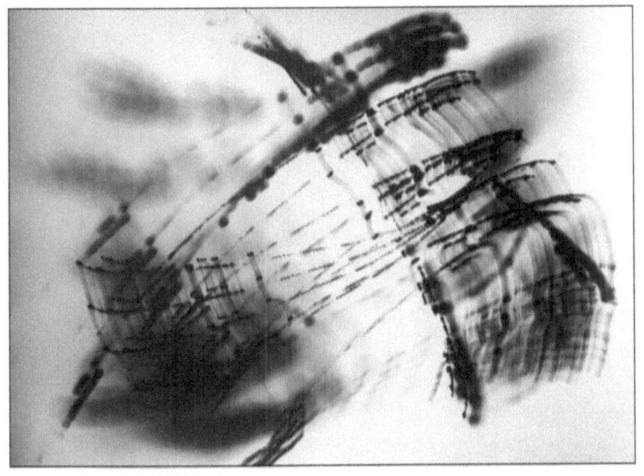

Adrienne Rich is Six Years Younger than Me

Adrienne Rich is six years
younger than me.
She was born when I
was six years old
A sister I never had
A sister I only know
through her poetry.

I was born when the country
was optimistic.
She was born the year of the crash.
When I was twelve she was six.
We were held down by the Depression.
When I was eighteen and she was twelve
we were at war.
When I was twenty-four and she was eighteen
we dropped the bomb
on Hiroshima and were at peace.

Poets need to suffer
I thought when I was twenty,
grieve unrequited loves

Then I married
and all that came to me. But
marriage did not make me
a poet. It did make me sad.
The children born and dying
did give me pain and grieving.

She had one book published
before she married. I did too.
She had three children before
she was thirty. I did too.
One book after she was married

I did too. But she had many
more. I did not. She became
a lesbian. I did too.

I am grateful to my muscles
for not seizing the day
to my heart for not stopping
to my lungs for breathing
even when I forget about them.

Adrienne Rich's body is older
than mine. Her body demands
a wheelchair. I stride
through the stacks
this afternoon in the library
listening to others cough
clear their throats.
I haven't written anything to equal Adrienne
or had to endure pain like hers either.

Someone asked me
would I exchange
my life for hers if I could?
for her education?
for her honors?
for her diamond poetry?
for her wheelchair?
for twisted hands
and feet

No, no!
At 75 my feet and legs
hold me up, my hands hold
more than my ability
to write a singing line.

And yet. And yet.

After Glory Wore My Overalls to Read Poetry
On Stage with the Dancers

My overalls
will never be the same.
They have tasted
fame and glory.
They have been on
stage. Acted.
Danced. They have taken
bows.
       They sit in my
living room disconsolate.
Refuse my closet. Remembering
yesterday. Applause.

My overalls, blue and
white striped, I've been a
carpenter in, worn to haul
manure in, repair
cars, clean
stove pipe.
       They hung in my
closet with nothing to
do. Once they were worn to
town. But not by me.
They were unemployed.
Mostly retired.

Now when I wear them they dance.
Act. Speak poetry.
And take bows.

After Viewing the Quilt

I

She speaks of her
brother
dead these six
years
how
she
sewed with
other women
turning the
edges
of his
panel
[a sailboat
(the one
he built)
sailing
out
to
sea]
her
grief
shaking
her
voice.

II

I'm with you
in that
bedroom
and
you are

crying
shaking
stretched
on top of
me
head on my
shoulder
saying
he was a
sonafabitch
but no one
should die
of
aids.

Appearances

Fall, 1990

Nobody liked the Baptist, John.
Were probably glad when he had gone
On his way shouting, "Prepare the Way.
Repent. Repent." was all he'd say.
He was nothing pleasant to look upon
With his unkempt hair, dirty, long.
His clothes unwashed as he was too,
His eyes quite wild, a nut, they knew.
An unlikely herald for God to send
To announce his son, and that world, to rend,
But then God never seemed to care
About appearances or hair.

Nobody liked the Redwood Summer.
The kids were dirty, what a bummer.
They shouted that they'd come to save
The redwoods from an early grave.
Unlikely heralds much like John.
"Repent. Repent." the same old song
Sung by those with much to lose
To those who they had asked to choose
Between the five percent or none
Before that final choice was gone.
Sometimes our salvation and grace is
From highly unlikely places.

Bear

This old bear
storms the
pavement
red faced
furious
looking for
who knows
what.

Leaves
me sitting
eating a
banana
looking at
city trees
trucks street
lamps.
Listening
to geese
honking
birds
scolding
and somewhere
unseen a
pump
chattering.

This old bear
grim faced
eyes
popping
roars through
town

        cursing
luck love
politicians
other
        garbage.

Black Silk

Your black silk shirt
through which my fingers
caress your breast,
revel in softness
of silk, discover
round and firm
circumference and radius,
navigate, explore
the rising center.
Your words add to this journal
of being lost on a continent
never touched before.
We send back
plant listings,
sightings of forests, rivers
reports of fevers,
disorientations.
Your black silk shirt
and my explorer's fingers
scouting the silk of skin;
in me rises a fire
to match your flaming
wanting. My fingers
and my lips
tease you into ecstasy.
This continent we explore
together. Our nerve ends
send messages to minds
we have forgotten.
Waking
to touch, to longing
to worlds, unmapped
until now;
to mind's remembering silk.

Borsalina Hat

I want a Borsalina hat.
Blue as the ocean
Shaped by loving hands
Soft but firm, riding my head.
Expensive. Very. But no more
Than what I pay for paper
50 sheets of 16" x 20" glossy.

I want a Borsalina hat.
Which says subtly I am upper class
I have been to Italy
To Borsalino and bought a hat
Even though I've only been to Old Town
To a boutique on Second Street
In sleepy Eureka.

I want a Borsalina hat.
To wear above my ravaged face,
To wear with my new long hair
Still brown with just a bit of gray.
To laugh at death
And be immortal. To make eyes turn
With shock and disbelief.

I want a Borsalina hat.
The melody of Borsalino
Sings in my ears,
Brings to the mind Mediterranean skies,
Wharves where ships wait
To leave on journeys
Into centuries still unborn.

I want a Borsalina hat.

But can I afford it?
Will I have to buy clothes to match?
And shoes? Where will I wear it?
To concerts? Art openings?
Will it change my life?

I want a Borsalina hat.
I could bring it home wrapped carefully
In tissue. Store it on my closet shelf.
Get it out at night. Wear it
To watch TV. Look at myself
In the mirror. Draw the drapes
And walk around the house, naked.

I want a Borsalina hat.
To wear carelessly
As though indulgent parents
Gave me a generous allowance
And trips to Europe
To Paris, London, Rome
And Borsalino.

Celebration for a Menarche

Come into the loving and welcome of women,
Bring your bloodstained hands,
You are strong in your blood's connection,
You are a woman among women.

Come into the loving and welcome of women.
Be born into your own birth.
Be born from this moment into your own life.
You are a woman among women.

Come into the loving and welcome of women.
Come with your bloodstained thighs.
You are fierce in your blood's connection,
You are a woman among women.

Come into the loving and welcome of women,
Our daughter, our sister,
Be born again in the love of our arms.
You are a woman among women.

Come into the loving and welcome of women,
Be born to us in your blood.
Dance in its radiance, dance in your passion.
You are a woman among women.

Come into the loving and welcome of women.
You are the creator.
You are the mother of your being.
You are a woman among women.

Coming Out

Will I have an empty space
where she has filled my arms?
Will there be a blank place
where she smiles?
Will there be only silence
where once I heard her voice?
Will it be as though
my daughter died?

Yet here are all my sisters
who live deceptive lives;
who lie to live,
who live to hide
who hide to eat, to love.
And here beside me now
the woman whom I love
who warms me, who I struggle with
who shares her love with me.

How can my sisters suffer
and I go free? And I go free?
But will I hear her voice again?
What will this mean to me?
What will this mean to her
my daughter? My sisters?
What will this mean to me?
My sisters. My sisters.

Confession

I am addicted
to chocolate
covered
graham
crackers.
Oh. Bring me some.
Yes. Those big ones
chocolate color
covering a tan
crumbly cracker
crunching
in my mouth.

Or those slender
small thin ones
mouthed whole.
I take my addiction
to potlucks,
celebrations,
receptions
to share. To keep me
from eating all of them.
At least all of that
pack.
Yes.
I need help.

I wake in the night
stumble into the kitchen
reach into cookie
jar.
I stash extra
supplies in the cupboard

the linen closet
under the couch.
I
drive to 7-Eleven
at midnight.
I dream
of chocolate covered
graham cracker
houses. I eat
the roof, the walls
even the path
chocolate colored
leading up to the house
even the chocolate
trees.

My friends try to help.
They suggest other
addictions: smoking
coffee cocaine
but none of these
work.
Oh bring me
chocolate covered
graham crackers.
Yes. Those big ones.
Yes.

Fire

Think of this move as fire,
Sudden, thorough destruction.
Destroying, cleansing,
moving into new life.
Green beginning to grow
in the foundations,
between the pilings.
            Think
of our parting as fire.
Our separation burning
our hands, our phones
in flames. Greening our
skins. The house
a cinder.
            Think of touch.
Stones and miles, limitless.
Ash on the wind. Loss
loss. Papers burned.
Chair and tables
tapestries and TVs
transformed.

Think of our fire as a move
bringing tender green shoots
of new love into our life
after the winter of absence,
the cold of dark. The rains
of spring surprising
green.

Think of fire come to us
as ancient sunlight
catching us in its grasp,

holding us firm as
lightening to earth.
                    Wildfire
burning us into wild flowers.

Forgetting

Sometimes I forget
I loved women.
Forget when we
loved each other
all of us
sisters
holding hands
in a circle
open to
each other's hearts
not as couples
but including
not excluding
other women.

Time has covered up
the touching
holding,
memory forgets
forgets until
a poet speaks a word.
Shocks me into
remembering
I did love.

How could I forget or you?
You who were my sisters.
How could we forget?
It has been a good day.
I washed my hair
cooked rice
called friends
sisterhood a distant
distant memory.

Greek Salad

Reds, greens, off-whites,
Blacks are a mélange of
Colors. Oranges too.
A painting or a poem
Good enough to eat.
So we do, looking
Into each other's eyes,
Laughing. Loving each
Other we illuminate the
Room. Our mouths
Sing. A melody of
Complexities. Our
Tongues dance among
Herbs and oils. We bite into
Smooth black olives.
Our teeth release
Subtle flavors,
Goat cheese, lettuce.
The crisp redness of
Tomato touching
Lips.

We are in Greece.
The temples of women
Rise everywhere.
In the mountain groves
By the ocean cliffs.
There is music
Women make and
Dancing. We nourish
Ourselves on light.
Flavors of reds, greens,
Orange, black, off-whites

Sing in our mouths.
We worship in our own
Image. Artemis, Aphrodite,
Hestia all ourselves.
We are surrounded by
Images… twelve toned
Composition…in an
Ambience of light.
Eating this salad.
Toasting each other.
Santé!
Santé!

Hitchhiker

People have been going through depressions for years.
And she had been having one. I was too.

I said to the goddess
when I woke up that morning,
if there's any woman
hitching, I'll pick her up.
So she took me at my word
and as I came out of Trinidad
there she was, my hitchhiker
my grown older hippie
my bag lady.
     She had two bags
one smallish, the other
smaller. She clung to that one
even when we got out to stretch.
     She didn't say much, just
something about adjustments
in her life and making new ones.
I said I was too.
     Her dress was down to her
ankles. She was wearing all
she owned. Travelling light.
I remember the astringent smell
of patchouli.
     Her face was strong. She
looked angry sometimes.
I played the flautist Rampal and
the baroque of Pachelbel
on my tape recorder.
     She looked out the window at
California and Oregon.
Said she liked the music
enjoyed the ride. Didn't like

to hitchhike but everything was
so expensive. Wanted to know if
Grants Pass had welfare. Oh, yes, I said
and dropped her at the office.

Is the goddess a hitchhiker?

I Remember

"It is marvelous to wake up together."
—Elizabeth Bishop, *Edgar Allen Poe & the Juke Box*

I remember waking
Next to you
Stretching sleepily
Turning to kiss you
Hearing the ocean waves
Kissing the shore
Sharing the morning
It was marvelous
To be near
Next to your body
Feel your arms
Around me.

Now I can only dream
No one to wake to
Being old
Being alone
Sharing with no one
My morning
My arms
My bed.

In My Aunt's Kitchen

The acrid smell of
steel knives, forks,
spoons with yellow
bone handles returns me
to that kitchen.
My aunt and I
cleaned them with sand
pushing the steel down and
up and down again and
again in the old
coffee can.
      The great black
coal burning cook stove with its
hot water compartment pies
baking in the oven soup
bubbling on the back of the
stove bread rising in
compartments above the
cooking space.
        The zinc-
lined box that holds the
dish pan adequate for
every day but not for
Sunday dinner.
          Leftovers
carried down to the cellar
to hanging shelves screened
in against the mice
the tablecloth removed the
Sunday dishes scraped and
stacked my aunt her
sleeves rolled halfway to her
elbows her large apron

over her Sunday dress
presiding over two large
steaming dish pans one
soapy water one clear while
she washes and other
aunts dry.
          The uncles
having retired to the
parlor to gather around the
radio in winter or the
long L shaped porch to
smoke or chew in summer.
I sit in the kitchen rocking
chair holding the current
cat on my lap listening to my
aunt assessing the week's
community news who was sick
who would need taking care of
who had eloped who was
pregnant sometimes the same
person who was down on their
luck could use some
extra food whether the
minister's wife who had
a large family could use
some help.
          Sunday dishes
dried stacked returned to the
walnut sideboard waiting
behind closed doors for
another Sunday dinner funeral or
wedding.
          On weekdays

sturdy white ironstone china
washed in the kitchen
zinc lined wooden
box.
    My aunt's begonias
lining the kitchen bay window
the small table covered with
plants and magazines. Two
rocking chairs. My aunt in
one. Her friend in another
talking having a piece of
pie or cake fresh from the
oven. The sun warming the cat
stretched out on the braided
rug.
    The smell of steel
knives my madeleine.

Inventory

Returning
from a trip
to my other
life
I bring
with me
hiking boots
thick wool
socks,
my grandfather's
tobacco jar
carved
from a tree,
three winter
watch caps,
three linen napkins
with mouse dirt,
the 1932 *Book Of Formulas:*
Recipes, Methods
And Secret Processes,
formulas
capable of destroying
or healing,
recipe for rat
poison,
lotion for poison
ivy....
one black pair
dress tuxedo
trousers,
one personal
electric fan,
two rare

books,
motorcycle
helmet,
oversize
hand knit
sweater,
gray
black and red
Indian rug
woven in the Southwest
bought by my missionary
uncle
for my mother,
brought by me
from Philadelphia
and yet another
life
one brown with white
stripes
some moth holes,
finely knit
wool blanket
with memories
of me being gently
covered after falling
asleep on the living
room couch.

Inventory in the 21st Century

Surrounded
By
These
Twenty
First
Century
Toys:
Android
Minipad
Computer
Printer
HD
Radio
Nikon D3300 SLR

Me born
1923
The
Beginning of the
20th century
Alive in
2013.

One foot
In electricity
One in digital.

Surrounded
By books
CDs
File drawers
Hard copies
Flash storage

All unknown to me
At birth
Before drones
TVs
Microwaves
Refrigerators....

It's Raining in Portland

You tell me it's raining
under this blue blue sky
with its white half moon,
it's hard to believe.
I had seen you today in my mind
under hot sunny skies
but it's raining in Portland.

I tell you of dressed up dogs.
Of playing with sound.
Of conversations I had.
Of the colors I've seen
as I walked city streets.
Of your lecture tomorrow.
Of breakfast with a friend.
Of a party you went to,
homesick Easterners, you say.
I tell you how I missed the trees
and my friends, and the snow.
And it's raining in Portland.

A white white moon
is shining outside
not the usual fog
with no start.

Was the day sunny
here in Arcata
as the morning in San Francisco?
When 9 o'clock bells tolled
on a sunny Sunday
and we ate breakfast
in ambient air

laughter caught
in green branches.
The city before us
hot in the roaring morning.
And it's raining in Portland.

You were lying in bed
thinking of me
listening to the rain.
I was lying in bed
looking out my window
at red red flowers
and blue blue sky
thinking of you
waking under a blue blue sky.
But it's raining in Portland.

Not the quick hard Eastern rain
but an Oregon rain
steady and light, gently penetrating the trees
the roofs, the collar of your coat.
A rain to walk through
without a hat.
Not the winter rain
chill to the bone
damp on the walls
mold-growing rain.

You tell me of black days.
Of learning to live by yourself.
Of betrayals,
and that it's raining in Portland.

It's raining in Portland,
so soon it will be raining here.
We share the same skies

and the same weather
rolling in off the Pacific.
Oceanic orgasmic changes.

I listen outside my window
for the sound of rain
remembering Petaluma
the heat of the sidewalks
the five of us in the booth
of the restaurant talking
surrounded in the cool grotto
by four TVs, one in each corner
and the waitress apologizing.
We still had hours to drive
and it's raining in Portland.

The sun was hot
streaming into the car.
Three went to sleep
while the driver and I
kept watch, talked softly.
And I wondered how hot it was
in Portland, and if you were
out in it. But it was raining.

It was raining in Portland
and in San Francisco it was hot.
We sat on the grass
next to the water
under a burning sun.
Corinthian columns
towering over us
reflected in the lake
the water appearing
and reappearing
in the oblong. And she said

"You gotta be kidding. People
get paid for this!?"
I kept thinking of all the money.
She said, "People are starving
on the San Francisco streets
and sleeping in the parks
and thank goodness it isn't
raining."
But it's raining in Portland.

You say every time I tell
someone about my blackness
I lose them. They want only
my sun. My blue blue days.
I am afraid to tell you
of darkness so deep I cannot
see my way. I'm afraid I will
lose you. I say, tell me,
call me, tell me your weather
dark or light, wet or dry.
And you say it's raining in Portland.

I wake to the sound of tires
swishing by. Your weather
is here, outside my window.

Loving Myself

I am loving myself
and not just metaphorically.
Sensuously, and I would share
this circling of my fingers
on the back of my hand and wrist
but in this strange land I live in
no one is here to share.
Once you, poet, wrote of my strong
delicate hands and how
you understood my art.
Yesterday, the inquisitors
asked me about design
and I tried to answer
with my voice, when only touch
would do.
I am baffled
by words, to describe
the lines that interpenetrate,
that float and sink
in volumes and shading.
That swirl, mirroring
my anger, frustration
shock and love.
There is no language
that can replace finger trace.
No translation I can speak
to these blind men
so out of touch.
Today I stroke my pen
on paper, wishing
for a woman to caress,
to trace my fingers
in her hand. A Helen

learning the word for water,
blind and deaf
and mute, as I am
till released by touch.

Memorial Circle

We sit in a large circle
remembering.
I didn't like her
one woman says
beginning the celebration.
She was hard to get close to.
Other women, surprised
at such candor, nod.
Yes, she was difficult.

She was prickly.
Like a porcupine
she sometimes
rolled herself up.
Wanted to be
left alone but
only for a time.
Then she would call
as though nothing
had happened.

Some women found
her porcupine hard
to get close to. Some
ignored the spines,
went for the soft belly,
enjoyed her warm smile,
her fine mind.
She was a poet.

I barely knew her
yet in the two weeks
before she died she

kept asking for me.
Wanting me at her
memorial.

She had no family
another said. Her family
was this circle gathered
to remember. Others
invited to remember
chose not to come.
We sit on chairs
in the meadow
surrounded by tall trees,
bird song, soft breeze.
Your lover, who with others
cared for you while you
were dying, told what
a privilege that was
to watch your leaving.
You have been and still
are a warrior.

Your Buddhist friend
chants for you. Another
sets your singing bowl alive,
waves rising,
penetrating our bodies.

In the spirit of detachment
you give away your goods,
sign over your car
to your lover, everything.

In that spirit your lover
empties storage lockers,
spreads this largess

on the lawn and in the room
where you died. All of us
she told the circle
were to take whatever
we like. Did we take
what we didn't need?
Just to remember.

We have a potluck.
Far too much for the circle
to eat. We talk about
her life. Her twenty foster homes
before she was five. Her
restlessness, never settling
down until now.
Her famous I'm outta here
and disappearing only
to surface a year later.

Embarrassed
we settle into choosing
clothing, office supplies,
CDs, CD player, boom box,
a beautiful painted umbrella,
your meditation pillow,
books of poetry,
jewelry, Buddhas.
You have good taste.
Each woman selecting
what calls to her.

You wanted a Viking
burial. Your body strapped
to a raft, set on fire, and
pushed into the sea.
Instead we take your ashes

down to the ocean.
Nine remaining women
give your ashes
to the waves. Your tombstone
a heart drawn in the sand
to wash away in the tides.

But you have not died.
I learn more about you
every time I play
a classical CD. Every time
I pick up your green notebook,
use your scissors,
watch your videos,
pass the bulletin board.

No you have not died
though your spirit
has gone on
leaving three days after
your last breath from
your crown chakra.

You who were so distant
are now so close.

Morning in Portland

The motorcycle
like an alarm clock
begins to shout.

I turn lazily
in the sun
into the arms
of my lover
swimming in a sea
of warm blankets
and thinking
of breakfast.

In other rooms
other women
turn in each
other's arms
warm and tender
protected
for a time
from the angles
and sharpness
of men's
world.

The mother cat
comes
complaining
of kittens
and breakfast
sitting next
to the electric clock
and eyeing

the blue
parakeet.

The motorcycle motor
goes faster and faster
and fades
down the street.

Two mornings now
we have been awakened
by the macho beast.

I turn to my lover
settling my head
into her shoulder.
She kisses my hair.
The mother cat
goes off
to complain
in other rooms.

It is morning
in Portland.

We sit in the kitchen
eating granola and milk
sharing an orange.
Women
sleepy and tousled
make coffee
on the white
gas stove
murmuring confusedly.

I clear the table
of beer bottles
and glasses
and leftover flour
from a pie
we all shared.

We wash the dishes
together.
We are still safe
with each other.
There are no men
to laugh
tell jokes
or vent
their own anger
on us.

Not yet.
This world
this culture
we understand.

We do not have to explain
to each other
this morning in Portland.

Mrs. Koch and Mrs. Frederici

This poem is really
not about them.
It is about my mother
and her love for women
and her staying married
until her death.

I can see us now,
my mother and me,
in Mrs. Frederici's kitchen
involved in a lovers' quarrel.
Mrs. Frederici as cold
as any lover I have ever known.
My mother bewildered, in tears.
What had she done wrong?
I am five, fierce to protect
my mother and helpless.
These two, living on either side
of this twin house. Did they
resolve the quarrel? Or did
they coldly nod to each other
while hanging up the wash?
Did my mother reach out
only to be rebuffed?
I can't remember.
I only know the inside
of the Frederici's house was forbidden
to me. I only see the angry
kitchen.

Later I am nine.
I am sitting on Mrs. Koch's porch
with my mother. My father

has dropped us off to visit.
Gone off on business. We live
outside of town now. It is
lonely for my mother. As we
sit, swinging in the glider,
there is a strange feeling
in the air. Mrs. Koch
is telling my mother
she has a new friend
up the street.
She doesn't want my mother
to visit so often.
My mother is shocked, hurt,
wants to leave right then,
but can't. My father is not here.
My mother, who loved women,
forced to sit, humiliated
on Mrs. Koch's front porch
'til he appeared. My mother.

Nothing You Can Give Me

Nothing you can give me:
tapes, records, photographic
paper, can fill the
space you hold in my
heart. That space you are
leaving, moving out of.

From now on it will be
letters not lunches
perhaps phone calls not
hugs.
	I have been
through this before. My
friends do not die they
move away leaving
me to grieve to wonder
at the emptiness to carry
this heavy knowing.

You do this to me now
excited about strange
skies a different
air new friends.

On Being Invisible

At first I thought a
blank piece of
paper would
do.
      A large expanse of
white   signed with my
name.
      You know me but
you do not know me.   I
am who you accept: woman
divorced many years
ago; mother of three   many
years ago; grandmother.

I tell you of women I have
loved. I say she. What do
you hear? How do
you translate this pronoun into
heterosexuality? How do
you ignore who I am?

My husband women say   stroking the
melody. Emily knew what was
unacceptable as did May Swenson
May Sarton   Adrienne Rich
Audre Lorde   Muriel Rukeyser.
Elizabeth Bishop lived with a
woman companion eight years.
All we hear about is
Robert Lowell. Frieda Kahlo had many
lesbian lovers. All we know is
what's his name. Willa Cather
called herself William. Lived with
women all her life.
      I am tired

of this invisibility   and angry
of ignoring ignorance
of the arrogance of passing.

I am lesbian as was
Virginia Woolf. But you say
she was married. So was
I. So was Margaret Mead.
I could go on   name you
poets you don't know or do
you? Judy Grahn   June Jordan
Mini Bruce Pratt. Her poetry is about
hiding as I did and losing her
children as I did not.

You say
What does it matter who they
are? They are poets.
But it does. It does.
They live half
lives.
Half poets
Half accepted
perhaps even less since they are
women too.
You live your lives
perhaps not accepted
because   poets
but we share that.
You pass as
men and
women.

Packages

You arrive
carrying
packages of
anger
deposit them on my
floor too
tired to
hold them
anymore.
Some are
scuffed the
brown paper
torn in places
others are
new
fresh off the
television
radio
newspaper.
Injustices
sealed with
shiny
tape
crisp brown
paper.
You leave
do not take your
packages with
you.
They
accumulate on my
living room
rug.
What

am I to do
with these
packages
not even
addressed
to
me?

Pears and Cheese

Women who loved me
brought me pears
and cheese. Hard pears
only ripening with time.
We ate the cheese.

Women who loved me.
Took me to their beds.
Me, the wandering lover
ripening with time,
and patience.
Eating the pears.

Women who loved me
brought me wonder
touching inside me
time ripening
impatience ripening.
Pears and cheese.

Portrait

My aunt, now eighty-one,
Seamstress to many
Nurse to even more,
A good kind forthright friend
In this small quiet town,
Preserver of peaches, apples
Vegetables and good grape wine,
Who knows no waste;
Childless, because she raised so many children,
Sat in her best bedroom,
A beautiful quilt
In her still supple hands
And said, if she had had her way
She would have been a man.
When they come in the house
They can sit down,
A woman has always got something to do.
(Her husband has one egg to find;
A large garden he summer harvests.)

"Still," she says, folding up the quilt,
"Since I wasn't born a man
I wasn't going to act like one.
I set myself to be a woman."

Her house immaculate.
Eight jars of peaches
Glowing on a shelf,
Her flowers many-colored
In the sun.

Reading Judith Barrington While Eating a Peanut Butter Sandwich & Drinking Milk in Tangren's Kitchen at Ten o'Clock in the Morning in Ashland, Oregon

Fresh ground peanut butter on my
favorite bread, Oroweat 100% Whole Wheat.
Bread I first met in a commune
twenty years ago.
I sit in the
rocking chair rocking back and
forth a blue napkin on my lap.
In my left hand Barrington's
poems in my right a handmade
cup blue striations white inside
with milk. Reading Barrington
her geographies and histories;
responding with mine. My dead
buried on commune land. Her
dead on foreign soil under
blackberries. My history lesbian
as hers. My dead under blackberries
too? The bones softening
as she says they ought in the
decaying wooden box like
chicken bones? Softening in the
pine box his lover made for him.
David he carved on the wooden
board, lifting the wood into
leaves. Making art for the
artist David was.
David
beautiful David. Men sought him out.
Told me proudly they were his
lovers. David driven by anguish for the

world. Obsessed by Dostoevsky's
Christ. Obsessed by death. Choosing
rope.
David
my son.

Remembering 1945

I have been thinking of you and me.
Those two young beautiful classic faces.
Those lovely bodies looking at each
other.

    I am listening to music.
The piano in my aunt's apartment
forty-five years ago, in a tree lined
street, high in all that green.

    I asked you to visit, you who
I wanted to be a man for so my love
would be acceptable.
I wanted to
tell you my love
Did my eyes tell you?

I would marry, as you would marry.
Have the acceptable number of children as you.
Missing a life

I only knew I loved. But you were right.
This was not acceptable. They only wanted us to marry
    replace   the dead, get ready for the next war.
    They   did not care about us. But I did and do.
    I   care for this waste, this loss. What we could have
    given   each   other.   For I know you loved me too.
    I   could see it in your eyes. But there was no
    name   for this. In our lexicon

    I   wonder, are you still alive?
Do   you ever think of me?   Would I
recognize that beauty now?

Are you divorced as I am? Are you a lesbian?
Are you a grandmother? Are all your children
alive? There is so much I want to know
but may never know. You moved
to the inner city.
That was my last card. Thirty-five years ago.

I still think of you in my aunt's apartment
Your delicate hands. Our parting so painful I cannot
remember it.
After you left I cried in that bed alone, silently.
I could not even
share my grief, even with my aunt.
Especially
not with you.

Self Portrait

What shall I be homesick for
And where? For the house
By the creek where the Tiffany
Shade took fire in the anger storm?
Where the trees blurred in vertigo
As I was swung to safety
Out of the path of danger?

Or should this longing
Be placed in the house of grief?
The year of separation
My mother's neck stripped of bandages
Under the gooseneck lamp
The doctor checking the necklace
Where the goiter had lived
An incision almost totally round.
The house where bowls of blood
Stood at the side of her bed
The surgeons having pulled all her teeth
The house where my grandfather
Flooded the kitchen by stuffing
The toilet with newspapers.
The house where I began talking to myself
Sitting at the kitchen screen door.
I dream of this house
Where I cut my kitten's ear
And terrified of blood
Now that I knew, hurled it down
The cellar stair. Terrified too
Of being found out. My first
Experiment. I dream of the house.
I go back. I want to buy it
To live in it but somehow

There is always something wrong
In the house of grief.

Or would I return to the orchards?
The spring an ocean of blossoms,
And the house of my father's battering?
Where I escaped to walk the country
Lanes, alone, storing up in my heart
This poetry? The alchemical basement
Where I transformed myself amid
Distillations and evaporations
And my tuberculosis settled behind a
Wall. The house where I was
Always tired. The house of
Uncertainty, of hunger, of migraine
Headaches and damaged hearts.
The house of depression.
Would I return to that room
With my books, reading in my black
Wicker chair? Or the closet
Where I climbed the steps
To nowhere?

If my life were straight lines
I could move without
Twisting and turning
And avoid vertigo.

Or would I return to my college room
That two windowed corner
Of joy and loneliness,
That room where I exulted,
And was cast down by betrayal,
Where lines flowed onto paper
As poems wrote themselves before my
Eyes. Where my loves were intense
But hidden, and detachment

The watchword. Four years of
Dislocation in a war mad world.

Perhaps it would be
The town by the canal,
The bookstore and its owner
Mentor, who nourished me
With new ideas, thoughts, music
Educating me with her conversation
Finding me eager to learn
Of a four o'clock afternoon,
My teaching finished for the day.
Browsing in the wide-plank floored
Wooden shelved space the light
Filtering in through the lead glassed
Windows, touching small sculptures
And plants as I touched, reverently,
Those books shipped from England.
Read and frequently bought these
Poets, my salary going into books
Records. Here I walked on air. My
Paradise, this town. And in my room
Light and airy, sitting at my applewood
Desk writing incunabula, the beginnings.
I am twenty-two, trying to catch the
Ambience of this place, so old the
Streets are cobblestones. Washington
Planned his battles here, and ghosts
March down the streets. I am twenty-two.
In love with the place,
In love with life I walk
Ten feet off the ground.
And in my room late at night
I hear rats scrambling through
The walls or in the silence
Universes spinning.

Song for Clarissa

So old girl we are parting.
How many years, how
many memories, how
faithful you have been
to me. How many scrapes
have we survived together?

Spinning on black ice,
Being hit by a travel trailer,
Sideswiped by another car.
Hit by a stop sign runner,
Little dings when you
backed into a Cadillac.

What adventures, crossing
the United States five times.
Boston, Philadelphia, DC,
Ithaca, St. Louis, Denver,
Salt Lake City, Los Angeles,
San Diego, Portland, Seattle.

Women's lands, women's road.
Challenges to test your metal.
Now we are parting. This last
test too much for us both.
Both of us too old. Rusty
both of us. Farewell faithful friend.

Strawberries

Come here, she called
(the morning just begun),
come around to the back,
come look at the strawberries.

As I rounded the corner
there she was
naked to the morning,
to the strawberries,
and to me.

Come look, she said,
pointing to the beds
where rabbits had had breakfast
and left a token of their
appreciation.
Come, look at what
they've done.

Naked in the dawning morning,
the cool breezes
playing gently around her,
she came into my arms
for warmth;
kissed me
and scurried back to bed.

Naked in the morning.
Burned into my memory
among the strawberries
and the sunrise,
her body memorized in my hands.

Suicide Poem

1

Suicides go on living
until they die.
They go on eating,
and crying,
and sleeping,
or trying to;
they go on working.

They look just like
anyone else...

No one knows
when...

Suicides die
just like anyone,
only sooner.

2

Suicides look at grass,
trees,
and smell wild lilac.
Sometimes they feel
soft summer breezes
blowing across their faces
just like other people;
their senses as acute.

Suicides look at sunsets,
see stars,
write poetry
and plan how...

3

Suicides aren't
always thinking about
suicide.
Sometimes it's about
breakfast,
or their next photograph,
or the rug they're making
or a bath.

4

Suicides consider their
options:
rope, overdose,
bridges, swimming out
too far, cars...

5

Suicides' noses bleed.
They get cramps,
headaches, cancer,
heart attacks
just like everyone
else.
Most people are afraid
to.
It's so permanent.
Exploring new dimensions
is not their thing.

6

There is no end
until the suicide.

The Ballad of the Barn

Carmen and Jean decided
To build their goats a barn
One that would be sturdy
And also keep goats warm
Now who would they get to build it
Who knew how it should go?
They went looking for some sisters
To help their dream to grow

Up from San Francisco
Came Priscilla and Roseanne
Also Jean and Cece
To talk about the plan
Later joined by Connie
And later joined by Anne
To build together a structure
To show us that they can

First they built the foundation
Strong as it could be
Then they put the posts up
High as you could see
Then they lifted beams
As high as they had to go
Some were twenty feet off the ground
And raising them was slow

It took a lot of women
To shake that cement down
It took a lot of muscle
To get those posts in sound
With transit and with tackle
They built it from the ground

And people came to see that barn
From many miles around

*(Written "by Ruth of Mountain Grove" before she changed her
name to Mountaingrove - circa 1970s)*

The Child

What is a mother to do?
How can she penetrate
into a child's mind
and leave him
secrecy
the dark
he needs for growing
seeking:
finding?

The telephone
brought us news
of the child
who hanged himself
a child
making a man's
decision

how
being cut down
he floated
between living
and what we do not understand

that longest week
(a mother's year)

Who is to know
the mind of a child
and what
he dreams?
His life
is always

in his hands
to live
or not to live.
No one
not even God
steps between
(man and death)
this freedom
and here
there was no
grace.

What is a mother to do?
The child's loaned.
Both are imperfect
and what we
shut our eyes to
is death
waiting
at every turn
in every car
at the sudden curve
in every illness.
We can only watch
vigilant, even
though we sleep.
Slide
the oxygen tent
the pulmotor
the vaccine
the mold
the transfusion
between the child

and
death.

What is a mother to do?
A child must harden
and must compete.
How will he live
and make his bread
without the hostile push
of hate?

Some can only hate
themselves
and
hang.

The Necklace

October, 1990

You brought me this finely threaded
sparkling glass from Venice, blue
as your eyes, as the skies
over the canals. I wore it
around my throat, the glass
matching my eyes. My piece
of Venice.
　　　Venetian glass.
Tiny pieces of glass, hundreds
strung on fine wire. Delicate.
I would hold it in my hands re-
membering you. This was a love
gift, though you would never
call it Eros. That part was for men.
Yet you did love me, as I loved
you with passion. And when you
spoke to others, they said pity
she's so young. This is mother/
daughter/Demeter/Persephone,
otherwise, Jung's women said, ideal.
And so you moved back. You
did not want to be my mother, nor I
your daughter. You had a daughter.
I a mother. Jung's women confused this
love. And Freud's men too. When you
went to him to talk about me
he said lesbian. This is lesbian.
Give it up. And so you did.

We were both married. What was he
afraid of? And what were you
afraid of? Because you were

afraid. Or why ask others?
I wanted you and yet I was
afraid. To tell you would be
to lose you? I would not risk
this.

Gradually the Venetian necklace,
blue as our eyes, came apart.
I kept, may still have it, somewhere
in Oregon, in a white box, in cotton,
but I think not. I think I have only the
memory of sparkling sky blue Venetian
around my neck. In your
hand.
    And only the
memory of you, dead now these
many years. Jung's women were
right, you were too old for me.
I would outlive you. Yet I have
known young women, twenty years younger,
as lovers. I have not been
too old nor they too young. Nor
would we have been, if we had had
courage.
    I have not forgotten you.
You are as much my lover as any
lover I have had. And Freud's men
were right. I am a lesbian.

To Nancy in Mexico

I lie by the open
window   sun streams through the
screen.   Steam rises from my
oatmeal   in smoky white
curlings.   The dark blue
bowl   reflects   sun.
                    Your
letter   rests   on   my
breakfast   tray   black
ink   on   yellow   lined
paper.   You tell me of
your sister's operation.   You say
your male lover has disappointed
you.   You tell me how you could
live out of a car.   That the
cat has six new
kittens.
        You tell me I am a
friend and sometimes a
lover   in a sense few would
understand.   It is not
sexual but passionate.   We are two
women in friendship.   You can
tell me anything   magic   or
mean.
        I remember how we made
love in the middle of the
day on Moonstone Beach surrounded by
families.   Two women   laughing
touching   reading   our
poems to   each other   our
hair mingling.
        I lie here   thinking of

you,   I do not tell all
I know.

        When you lived in
Fieldbrook   we woke on
Sunday mornings to
Nakamichi tea   a bowl of
fruit.   Pulled back
curtains to watch
birds at your feeder.

                        There are
always these possibilities between
us   friends.
            You sign your
letter
        love.

Valentine's Day

It's a clear day.
Sun just up over the mountain.
They call them mountains here
just as in New Jersey.
But I know mountains.

My neighbor is taking a bath.
Her water courses through our walls
drowning out the tape of love poems
I'm listening to. Thin walls,
like my apartment in Pennsylvania.
I turn up the volume
and my lover and friend's
voice fills the room.

I hear my neighbor
swishing her hand in the water,
testing its hot or coldness,
adding more cold or hot;
an intimate gesture,
close as the wall between us.

Like the Japanese, who live so intimately,
yet with rigid protocol, we have talked
twice since I moved here three years ago.
Once she asked me if I had ants in my bedroom,
and yesterday, if my cable TV was working.
I said I didn't have cable.

My lover's poems speak of longing,
of desire, of wanting, of loneliness,
of fantasies, of worlds we have yet to make
as women living in man's creations

like this thin wall between neighbors.
What woman, needing privacy,
would design such a wall?

My lover's voice tells of waiting,
of rejection. I lower the volume.
When my neighbor has friends
or relatives in her bedroom
or her bath, I can hear every word they say.
My lover speaks of divisions,
of distances, of cats with visitation rights
she doesn't have. Of how the city
splits her into more than one shadow,
more than one name.

My neighbor washes herself.
I can hear the slap of her wash cloth,
the roll of the water as her body moves.
We are like lovers
knowing so much about each other.

On the tape my friend and lover
talks of hunger, of wanting closeness,
of no food, of mist rising,
of being stopped in reaching out
by her own self, as I am.
A thousand miles of lonely
she says. My neighbor
makes breakfast in the kitchen,
I can hear her draw the water,
turn up her TV.

We are like lovers or roommates
accommodating to each other's sounds,

each other's ways of being.
But never talking to each other,
never saying that sound is irritating,
I wish you'd be more quiet.
Never. The tape talks of busted thumbs,
of separation, of aloneness.

My friend's voice reads me poems
of women she has known, of sisters,
and asks if we opened up our fists of rage,
our palms to each other, would that love frighten?
Would we draw back from such intensity?

My neighbor's TV murmurs in her living room.
I have made six phone calls this morning
still in my bed, the phone next to the wall.
Does she know I am going to San Francisco?
That I've got a ride one way but not the other?
That I'm borrowing a map?
That the woman I was going to go with is ill?
That I'm going with another?
That the woman I'm staying with
doesn't know whether I'm coming or not,
all of this only coming together this morning.
Does she know my uncertainty,
let's admit it, my scaredness
about getting around San Francisco,
alone, by bus; or is she only curious
about the ants in my bedroom?

The love poems speak of mothers
who do not mother. Of daughters
who do not marry doctors or lawyers
but become them, and the regret

of grandchildren unconceived,
and the voice that asks,
Why do you hate me?

I lie here thinking of laundry
knowing that is not the question.
The question is why do men hate women?
Hate them so much they would destroy the earth,
and themselves with it.

The poems speak of birth,
of labor, of loving the child
and the mother into life.
Of breach birth, the slowness
and then the urgency, the critical point;
the poem a manual of instruction.
And of death, and the quietness of blood.

There is quiet next door.
Has my neighbor gone out?
Is she taking a nap?
Is she reading in her living room?
Or watering her flowers?
Is she lonely?
Is she listening to my tape?

The poems speak of old friends
and old memories, of homesickness
for blue mountains. I know
that mountain chain. It stretched
up through my Pennsylvania childhood.
The poems speak to my own
wantings. The wanting of closeness
and independence, the wanting of intimacy

and distance. The dilemma
we stick on the horns of.

I do my laundry, my tape recorder
on pause.
        The poet speaks
of committing a relationship
like committing a murder
or committing suicide. I have
never thought like this....
Of murder, yes. Of suicide, yes
but not of committing a relationship.
What would that mean?
An action? A doing to?

I make lunch, put my laundry in the dryer,
come back to the poet
speaking of right brain being
unencumbered with linear.
I am gathering my books and papers.
At some time tonight I will be
the blind violinist, so I take my violin.
Yesterday my doctor predicted
my eye would veil to the point of operation,
giving me two years as she saw it.

My lover/friend talks of Brandenburg.
Of packing her life and leaving
and of learning that we never leave
even if we never go back.

And what of my neighbor you ask,
what is she doing now?
There is a clicking

on the other side of the wall
as though bureau drawers
were opening and closing.
Is she looking for ants?

My lover/poet speaks of colors.
Red and yellow, and of love
that ferments in the secret test tubes of time.
Of how she finally understands
my art. My neighbor bangs the door,
turns up the TV,
yells into the phone.
I am not interested in what she says,
though once she goddamned
someone from the living room to the bath,
furious and raging,
shaking my own centeredness,
remembering in my bones
my own rages, so distant
now I live alone.

Part Three

Time & Aging

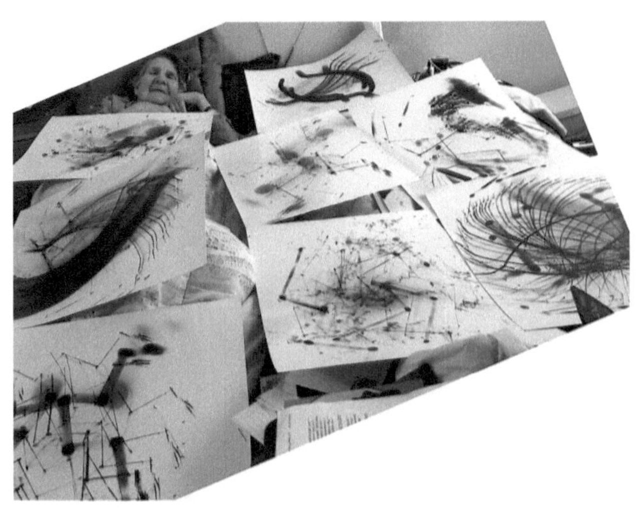

??????????

Am I out of my mind?
At my age - a bicycle?
Am I looking for
broken bones?
A crushed skull?
Do I want people
to take care of me?
Is this my answer
to not driving a car?
Is it Spring?

Do I need
training wheels?
Do I need
a helmet?

Do I need
my head examined?
Is this madness?
Do I need
a psychiatrist?

Do I have the courage?

4 am

It is 4 am
outside the windows
dark blue sky
begins to lighten.
The hospital
awakes, ready
for the day shift
at 6.

I am in my bed
singing the morning
into the world,
singing softly
"Morning has broken
 Like the first morning.
 Blackbird has spoken
 Like the first bird."

Two nurses stand
transfixed in the doorway,
the song so unexpected
in this quiet hour

Praise for the singing,
Praise for the morning....

At Ninety

so you're
90
So what
so you've lived
90
years

Lucky you
Breathing
Eating
Defecating
(fancy word)

Still got
Your mind
What's left
What's right
Lucky You
Ungrateful You
Envied

Maybe

Didn't ask
To be
90
But here
I am

You

Are

Others
Like
You
90
too

Fetus

Let me be
Let me be a fish, a bird
Let my heart return
To my dreaming body.
Let me for a leaf of time
Fall back into silky darkness.
Let me be a seed,
Let my brain be my seeing
Let my feet be gills or wings
let me find a different medium
let my beginnings go down
Sweet, loose, clean
Be stream riffle, pebble roll
into a vastness of salt
rubbings of sand
let me come again
free of time's forceps
glare and noise
measuring and weight
no mouth to cry
let me slip this skin
so you may bury
my placenta
bloody with beauty
an almost child.
let me enfold into
a new becoming
a whisper, a rustle,
a singing toad,
sounding
for small things
tender me!
surrender me!

Fresh

No one will replace your lost
childhood. No one can.
The secret is to
build another story more to
your liking where the
sun shines more often
birds sing more sweetly
rivers run sparkling to the
sea.
      Where fruit hangs
ripe for small
hands to pick.
      Where your
mother enfolds you in
love. Your father is
always there but does not
molest you.
      This is a
world you can build now
out of your own desires.
Fresh green trees. Fresh
bodies always clean sprung
like Venus from the bath. A
world wrapped in Mozart
Schubert Schumann Berg
Schoenberg Weber.
          Safe
serene where you will
your will.

Her Life

She is eighty.
The four of them
will hold a family
council   with
her.

They will ask
what do you want
to do with your
life?

     She is eighty
her body has problems
she does not want to
move.

     She lives alone
in her own house
she does not want to
move.

They will ask
what do you want?

     She
is no longer useful
cooks no longer   nor cleans
needs someone else
to do it for her.

They will ask
what do you want to do?
What do you want to do
with your life?

Holding court

expecting her to give in.

>   Hasn't she given in
all her life
to parents
to husband
to children?

And these
are her children, asking.
Underneath their question
is do you want to die?
Do you want us to help you
die?

>   She hears few choices.
The nursing home where
three years should be enough
to kill   or we can arrange
an overdose   if that's your choice.

The children lead
complex lives with little time
for her even though she gave
years and years.

>   She is
eighty.

And they ask
what do you want to do
with your life?

I Have Nightmares

I have nightmares of incontinence
Where all my carefully unsaid
Streams out through my gaping mouth
Volcanoing from deep deep down
Where I have stored all the hurts,
The wishes, the might have beens
My tongue speaking on and on
Shouting of truths
I do not want to hear or know
Or mumbling incomprehensible words
I do not understand.
No. No. I did not say that.
My lips, moving, moving.

I have nightmares of senility
Where my pen runs on
Filling the paper with confusions
Filling the paper with insanities
With incomprehensible words
Writing whatever it wills
Dropping out letters and making new
        ones.

I watch my hand
Disconnect from my brain
Take off on its own.
No. No. That is not what I meant
To write. No. Not this linear
Scribble, even I its creator cannot
Read.

I have nightmares of being toothless.
One by One I pull my teeth one by one

Cavern, my words, gibberish.
I smile an empty smile.
In dreams my teeth are many pieces
Fitting inside each other
Effortlessly flailing from my gums.
In dreams I am horrified.
How will I speak or sing?

I Know What I Saw

I see them
at the foot of my bed
in stair steps
the tallest,
the second
the third
five of them
as they march
out the door
close it
followed by
the tallest shadow
the second and third
till five of them
catch up
and are gone.

"Oh, yes", the nurse says,
 "people in ICU
have frequent
hallucinations"

But I know what I saw

I look in my mirror and see my age

looking
back skin
around eyes
shrinking eye
brows no longer a
neat line teeth
considering
unfaithfulness
my grandmother's
profile quilted
cheeks a mole
hair that keeps
growing my forehead a
crisscross of
lines
in my eyes
broken red lines and in
hiding an incipient
cataract to veil my
world
my hair
still mostly brown
my hands still mostly
young my body
too
my face
my age

Invitation

As though someone knocks on
every door. My throat. My
ear. My gut. My head. My
heart. Seeking
entry. Testing this
house for sturdiness, for
solidity. Checking the
basement and the
roof. Let me in. Let
me in. No, not by the
hair of my chinny chin
chin.

    Old Death
I know you wait for
me, perhaps
impatiently. But do not
come too soon. Do not come down the
chimney. I will have boiling
water waiting.

    No, wait till
I open the door. Have the
table spread with
food. Wait till you are a welcome
guest. Candlelight, music, wine.
Come as a lover, not a building
inspector. Bring flowers.
Wear your tux.

Memory

It's memory
that makes me tired.
All those packets
of remembering
waiting, pushing
facts I've forgotten
wanting in, into now
dragging like Marley
chains of joy and hurt.

It's dates and times
almost lost now forty years.
It's being flooded with images
with women's voices
women's energy.
Women finding their power
their strength.
Women finding themselves.

It's memory
that overwhelms me.

Sometimes

I want to
lock the door
walk away
disappear
start over again
in a strange town
with new people
to be discovered.

Want to lock the door
and walk away
from piles of papers
magazines. books
mushrooming
taller and taller
overflowing desks
chairs. tables.

Want to walk away
from all my children:
poems. paintings. photographs
videos. computer disks
crowding closet shelves
tops of bureaus
wall space
cabinets.

Want to disappear
from invitations
opportunities
knocking loudly
promises made
obligations
demands.

Start over again
new telephone number
new name
new landscape
new bank
new herstory
to carve out
in a new town.

A strange town
where I get lost
am lonely
find a new doctor
new mechanic
new grocery store
new gas station
a new me.

New friends
new challenges
new clothes
new thoughts
new time zone
new weather
new food
new past.

To learn
in that place
the invisible
connections
that bind the town
together

to walk lightly
as a stranger.

Sometimes I want
to walk away
leave dirty dishes
dust balls
under the couch
bulging wastebaskets
rugs asking for the vacuum
windows wanting cleaning.

Sometimes I want
to lock the door
leave behind
messages piling up
on the answering machine,
frost pushing out
the freezer door
the computer mute.

The computer
hundreds of messages
clogging my account
bouncing on the Internet;
notes from net friends
asking where I am
how was my weekend
how is my health.

Walk away from
classes
exhibitions

meetings,
meetings,
meetings.
Just lock the door
walk away.

Some days I want
to disappear
leave all the unanswered
letters falling off the bed table
sliding onto the floor.
Leave all the unanswered
questionnaires
to find their own answers.

Someday I will do that.
I will leave all this
magpie collection
that is my life
metaphorically speaking.
I will die. No metaphor.
Someone will sort through all this
wish I was alive.

Wish I was alive
and while they sort through
this magpie collection
I will be sitting
in my Mustang convertible
(I plan to take it with me)
on a comfortable cloud.
laughing.

The ICU

In the ICU
he dances for me
faun like.

We've met before
he tells me.

Two years ago,
I was in his
world.

I don't
remember.

He picks up
the rose, touches
it to his lips
holds it in his
fingers tips
delicate,
slender
as he is.

I photograph
him. Shyly he
turns his head
away.

I want to remember
him
when we meet
again.

This Old Lesbian Dreams

—for mezzo-soprano Frederica Von Stade

She sees this woman with blue eyes
short blond hair
come striding into her life,
so sure of what she wants
and what she wants is this
Old Lesbian. She opens her arms
to embrace her.
This Old
Lesbian, who can have any
woman she can imagine
dreams this dyke, black
trousers, fancy top, with radiant
face, holding her, kissing her.
Yes, this Old Lesbian can have it
all, all this radiance,
this marvelous energy. Yes
Even this love.
        They will never
misunderstand each other, never
Quarrel. She will make love
to this Old Lesbian and she will be
Loved. They are perfect for each
other. This blue-eyed, blond haired
Dyke, so sure of herself,
will always be true. Will always be
there whenever this Old Lesbian
imagines her.

Vampire

They praise me
for my veins
as they suck my blood
pricking my skin
with their needle teeth
with their satisfied faces
as they smile at me
filling their tubes
one, two, three, four.
Vampires in this world
where it is legal
to draw my blood
out of good veins.
Some of them are good at it,
some are not, their
marks purple
under the skin.
Praise me in song and
story for my good veins.

Visitation

They all gather round
At five o'clock in the morning
saying what about me?

All those men
and women
from the boy next door
to my last lesbian lover.

What a lot of them
I had forgotten:
the truck driver.
the psychiatrist,
the wholesale
antique dealer,
the doctor,
the railroad engineer
saying what about me?
Don't forget me.

The violinist,
The writer/photographer,
The pilot
The chemist

Don't forget
The philosopher
The social worker

Who would think
There were so many
But in a long life…

A rosary of names
Feelings
Long loves and short
Loves
Saying each name in my mind.

But what about me ?
You're forgetting
Me.

The opera singer,
The poet
Demanding memory.

Don't forget about me.
Don't forget about me.

When You Don't Eat

When you don't eat
For five days
You are sending
A message
When you are blind
Or almost. Only a slit
Of light touches you
Your owner tells me.

Your teeth are rotten
Bad breath.
When you are old
Then you are scheduled
For a final sleep
At two in the afternoon
No wandering off
To die in solitude.

She brings you
To me to say goodbye…
And when
And when I don't eat
For two weeks
Will I be sending
A message
Too

Will

Everybody should have one
I suppose.
A bringing together
of the current life
and a look into the future.

Depending on your age
you may be more or less
intimidated.
A will suggests
mortality. That you
will not be present
when it is read.

A will makes you
gather up those
strands
willy nilly.

You will find your self
cleaning out
all the cubby holes
of memory: the Chinese
poem you wrote for
a lover, your children
needing to be mentioned,
commitments you must honor.

You Just Can't

Stop
Me
From
Dying.

Not
All your
Pills
Your Caring
Your Food.

It is no
Way

Much
As
You might
Like
To keep
Me
Here,
The heart
Will have its
Way.

Much
As I
Might
Like
To
Stay
The
Heart
Will have
Its
Way.

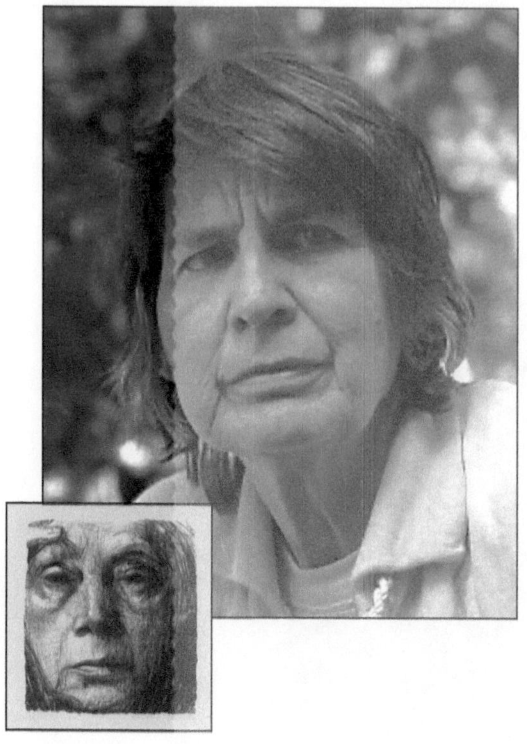

"For four years I thought about making self-portraits but somehow couldn't quite figure out how I wanted to do it. Or make the 'why' conscious. Then I read about Käthe Kollwitz and saw the self portraits she had made over the years. I saw how she recorded the changes in her being, inner and outer, as she grew older. I decided to make my own record. In enlarging the negative I close cropped the head, not only to emphasize the strength and determination I felt in myself, but also to produce an intimacy (all the crows feet and wrinkles). I have been making self portraits since my 56th birthday." —Ruth Mountaingrove, *The Blatant Image*, 1981.

Part Four

Disjunctive,
a Poem in 72 Parts

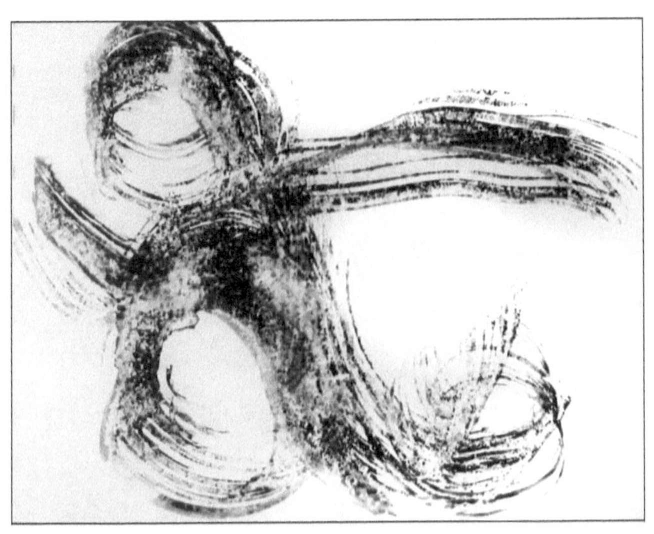

Disjunctive

Spring, 2013
1

I eat my way through
books   sometimes
a nibble here   a
bite there   random
and yet devouring
all the words before
I'm done.
        My eyes
protest   wave red
flags   warning me to
STOP.
            Enjoy   I say
but mind cannot rest
until it's eaten
all   all words
all sentences   all
pages.
        Then like
Psyche it can separate
chaff from grain. The
analytical ants march
soldier to each pile.

Enjoy I say   but
Psyche cannot rest.
She must spin the
chaff into gold
and tell her name.

II

I would want you only
if you were in love with
me.
        Not the sharpness of
you. Not the bitterness.
Not the cutting tongue.
        Once
I transformed you into
gentleness   with my
touch   my singing.
My scent calls
more to men than women.
They come sniffing about.
The women walk away
forget my address   lose
my phone number.
I put you down next to a
mall   satisfied now
that you would be fed.   I
forget where you
live.
        The teller asks for
my number   making sure
I am.
        I pay my bill in
cookies. When we meet
again I will owe you
three dollars.
        Poetry is an
expensive business.

III

This is all

rusted through.   No
wonder it broke in my
hands.
        I hear these words re
sound in my rusty
heart.
        Well   she said
we'll give you a new
one.

        Why don't you
write? Is it too hard to
start over?
        I kept both
your cards. You promised
to come back.

        The key to
anyone's history is their
childhood.

IV

Today the sun
shines as though it always
has.   But I know.
I can remember darkness
nights lit only by street
lights.   Days of pale
winter light with trees
that never drop their
leaves.   The coldness of
bone.

V

Soon I will begin the

day again. Rise from my
bed   wash and brush my
self   stack the dishes
transform eggs in flame
cover the bed with strange
birds from India.
         Keep
my promises   wondering why
you didn't keep yours.
         Promises
keep me going.   Otherwise
why get up?

VI

I could lie here
melting gradually into the
sheets   down through the
mattress pad   into the sponge
rubber   down into the
springs   into the tile floor
into the concrete slab   into
the bedrock.
         And when they
finally began to wonder   to
break in   there would be
nothing here but the
strange birds from India.

VII

How can I write
you   when there is no
address?

VIII

Going to another country
the traveler packs warm
clothes   and clothes for
cold   clothes for
rain   for sun   for
fog   for blistering
heat.
        The traveler
comes in quietly. Does
not disturb the dogs.
        When
she awakes there are strange
birds. Trees she cannot name.
A chill in the air.
        She is already
thinking of returning.
        Someone
has rearranged the room.

IX

You should not have written on
stone.
        How can I forget you
now?

X

When I said I
transformed
you   I meant
I uncovered what was
already there   but
buried by coldness
walls of mistrust.

XI

The police were here
last night   lights
flashing   saying:
you should know
this: the red light is
always on.
        The wall
is vibrating with
music.
        The bus
beeping   admits a
wheelchair.
        The
gladiolas are mostly
dead.
        It is a
gray day.
        I write
a letter in red ink to
you. Do not be
afraid. I am not
attracted to you.
        It is
the only pen I have.

XII

Really this is the only
way. What did
you
expect?
        Irritations
don't always make
pearls.

        I could love
you again.
        Don't take my
letters seriously. I don't
want you back.
        Habits
are hard to break. Relation
ships too. Sail yours
somewhere else.
        Don't
come knocking on my
door. Some one has already
eaten grandma.
        It is too late to
save the wolves.
        Why did you
ask me?
        There is
nothing I can say will change
your mind.
        I am a prisoner and
so are you. We have
nothing to give each
other.
        When I asked her
she took off her glasses.
The better to see me with?

XIII

Father   why are you
haunting me? I paid you off
years ago.
        You never did like
poetry. Send in your own
clowns. We will never be

friends. You will never
understand me. That's just the
way it is.
　　　Your world I
never wanted.
　　　My inheritance?
Peace you said but it is
not　　it's never over
over there　　or it seems
anywhere else in the
world　　not even here.
Peace　　with flashing
lights　　screaming　　bad
trips.

XIV

Green grapes call to
me　　remembering　　re
calling　　other summers
hot with desire re
minding.
　　　How different
this summer　　when you are
in Sweden. Incommunicado.
You tell me you will be
back in December.
　　　You
send me a postcard.

XV

People are learning how to
die now.
　　　There are so many of
us.

Young people are
learning to live day to
day with or without
memory.

XVI

She calls me. What can I say?
I have no cure. I am not a
doctor or a priest.
        The speakers
thump their heart music
earth
quaking the walls.
        When do
they ever sleep?
        What is in the
medicine cabinet? Is
someone sleeping in the
bathtub?
        Counselors can
influence your dreams. Every
Jungian knows
that.

XVII

The grapes are gone.
I have nectarines to feed my
soul and peaches.
        Far better than
words   and more filling.
        The
wind blows   tossing hair about
the sun shines. Hair and
flags   stream out straight.

              We
speak of you in the post office
a man between us. There is
always
a man between us.

XVIII

Now you are as
old as she   when you met
and she is
as old as perhaps
you may be   some day
but there are limits.
            I
have gone on with my
life and filled the spaces
I kept for you.
            I am not
allergic to cats. You can share
your house with
me.

XIX

You think it's easy
this fitting together all the
pieces. You never did
understand puzzles or
finish them.
        Someday
all of this will catch
you up. You will be
cold.
        Making the
frame is not

enough. It is the last
piece that completes.
Why can't you see that?
It is so clear.

XX

Waking to explosions
sound of fire   police cars
fire trucks   you
sonovabitch   a voice says
softly.
        I agree the voice says
on the other side of the
wall.

XXI

Because you could not
believe   you could not be
healed.
                My remedies
invisible to you.   No
cure for what you
could not feel.
        You
left us both bereft.

XXII

Father   these Indian heads
you saved   gleaming copper
or covered in verdigris.
Those arrowheads   chipped
stone   collected in your
bureau drawer. Those shapes

found while digging in the
garden   shaped into sharp
shinned V's. Collector's items.
You even gave me one.
Disembodied   no longer part
of the shaft   no animal
missed or
found.
      These were made by
flesh   bone   blood   hands.
You never told me that.
      My
Indians flickered on the
Saturday screen.
      We built our house
there.

XXIII

What do you convey as you
sit here   peeling skins off
onions   speaking don'ts
rules   expectations. What
is that smile for? Where
is your heart?
      You are always
afraid   seeing in every
trip   a car smash   a
plane crash.
      You
cannot enjoy the
journey   the scenery is
a green
blur   splattered with
blood.

XXIV

His black pickup
truck   hurtles toward
her.   Drunk at the wheel
he means to take
Persephone with him to the
underworld   but she escapes
into life. A different
story.

XXV

You take heart
medicine   but that is not
the same as love.
        You call
you say you don't know why
wonder if there is any good
loving sex   not likely
I say   you are looking
in the wrong place.
        He
wants to live with her again.
Some people never
learn.

XXVI

She calls me from across the
country. She is sending me a
book. It will have part of my
life in it and part of hers.

XXVII

I dream of her. She is my

lover again. I wake in
ecstasy.
    On the other
side of the wall   voices
murmur
questions   two guitar strings
break.
    In her office the
fax machine
wakes to ask
Where are you?

XXVIII

I have disappeared
onto the clipboard
invisible to your
eyes.
    My secrets
are   visible
paste.
    Look   my
life in glowing
color   right there on the
screen. Isn't science
wonderful.
    We bring good things to
better living through chemistry.
We care mostly for
money.
    She is dying of
cancer   not a good
thing.

XXIX

The sea affects the
sky   miles away   unheard
mostly   the colors remind
us   the wind carries
salt smell.
    Outside the
window   a Doppler
traffic   cars   trucks
approach   and   fade
away.
    An urgent
ambulance   punctuates.

XXX

You can give me
nothing   my closets are
full   and my
apartment.
    I would give
you something   but all my
good things are
worn out.

XXXI

The wrong number
gets me a connection to the
universe.
    On the other
side of the wall   rush of
water   a curse.
    And when I
hear you have died in a far off

place   will I remember
how you stroked my skin?
Or will I
forget?
        She calls
No   I am not she
I am not he.
        She
crosses my number off
her list.
        He calls   long
distance   asking for
who I am not. A
mistake   he says
a three not a two
I'm sorry.

XXXII

The helicopter
man   looks in gardens
searching for   misdeeds
felonies   among the
tomato plants.

XXXIII

She tells me inanimate
objects can come
alive   like Pinocchio.
I remember when the
fireplace   moved into my
eyes   when sounds
came apart   like
disengaged   railroad
cars   when green was

terrifyingly   alive   when
I decided to live.

XXXIV

On the other side of the
wall   men move about.
Outside   it is still
black.
        Convergence of
sirens disrupts the night.
We gather on the sidewalk
but see no flames. Dissolve
back into our apartments.
Comfort ourselves with
TV   wait the 11 o'clock
news.
            How often
I wanted to tell
you   but I was
afraid.

XXXV

Stress   lives with
me   an uneasy
companion   threatens
paralysis   and
vertigo.
        I move
cautiously   do not
make   sudden
demands   remember to
breathe.
        A period   put
carefully at the end of a
sentenced life.

XXXVI

At dawn
trash trucks collect
discards   garbage   old
envelopes   rumble
compressing   what they
find.
      I collect
letters   I may never
read again.
          She tells
me   we must meet for
coffee.
          She forgets to
call.

XXXVII

Old ladies get up
wander about at all
hours. They have no
boundaries. He is no
longer there to call her
back to bed. The
children   sleep in their
own houses.
      The heart beats
two and a half billion
times in a life of
seventy years.
          Turn on the light.
Make night into day.
          Read
she advises   wash
your kitchen floor.

You are awake.
Don't stare at the ceiling
in the dark. You live alone.
Enjoy it.   Get up.
Make yourself a
cup of tea. A piece of toast.
Your own
life.

XXXVIII

The avocado tree
drops one nine-leafed section
with a thud.
The spider is large with
child. She is not
Charlotte   and seems
annoyed   having to flee
my heavy-handedness.
Pregnant   she wants
only to repair her web and
wait. She has made a poor
choice. This is my
door.

XXXIX

A guitar
plays in the next
room. It is four
a.m. No moon.
          A
car alarm   screams
undulating the air.
A man's figure
runs across the lawn

slams the cab door
U-turns the truck
disappears into the
night.

XL

He tells me he is
going through changes
is tired of being poor
wants a real job with
real money.
    I only asked him
how he was doing.
        Whatever
happened to fine?

XLI

The tractor lawnmowers
past my window   rattling
the glass.
The driver's eyes
cast down.
      The
sun is visiting.
    At night
monsters walk across
my windows.
       Frontier
now means exploring the
mind.
      Monsters wait there to be
found by those driven to
know.   The executioner
the doctor   the savior

the humorist.
     Beware of the
humorist. She can destroy
you with a laugh.

XLII

Words move though my
head   looking for a place to
lie down.   I am tired of
supporting them. Why don't
they get a job   find a place to
live   like a dictionary or a
spell checker.
     Work for
witches   mumbling
incantations.

XLIII

This is a large world for a
three year old. Trees
stretch far above her
head. Cats impose.

XLIV

Mirror   mirror
who is the sanest?
who is the savior?
who will rescue us from
ourselves?
     The quality of
mercy   can be strained
indeed.
          Where is your

panacea? Can't
you do more
than
reflect?
        When I look into
you   all I see is
myself.

XLV

The mice are in the
corner   the fodder's in the
shock   my mind is on
computers.   I believe
I believe   in transparency
in electricity   in being and
nonexistence.
          I will call
up my memory. I will
save. I will believe. My
words are there   somewhere.

XLVI

Vertigo   vertigo
wherefore art thou
vertigo?
        Are you from the
mill I can see
belching smoke   into the
foggy air? Am I breathing
that formaldehyde?

Sun cuts through
lighting the room   clearing
the air   clearing my head.

XLVII

What dreams am I made of?
Cat's whiskers? Old bedding?
Violin strings?
        The poet says
you can't help but be original
if you are true to your self
but was he? true to self?
original?

XLVIII

What wells up
out of the depths? Was it better
left there? Who is this
woman who deserts me?
The mercy of man
kind is not. But
mercy me what of
woman?

XLIX

Buy this genuine ten carat
rhinestone from the
Nibelungen.
        Be the first in
your neighborhood to flash
this ring.
Yes   that has a ring to it.
Let's watch Valhalla go up in
flames.
                        You be Brunhilde and
I'll be Siegfried   unfaithful
to my sister   victim of the

flaming rhinestone.
      Or you be Vita
I'll be Virginia.
      We'll both be
Orlando.

L

She brings me
apples from the Trinity
Mountains   eight acres of
orchards and no one to
eat them but the
horses.
      Shocked at such
waste   when homeless
people are starving.

LI

Men want it all   he said.
Other men   women
children   even
animals   when you're
king   who can refuse
you?
            Women
really only want
women.
      Kings find this
chilling.

LII

If I had a modem
I could find you. I
could confirm you
exist.

LIII

A smell of
green comes in the
window.
     Sounds of
water.
     My memory
seeps back   rising in the
layers it has sunk
into.
     I scrub this
stone clean. It
persists.
      I keep
appearing   like a
ghost   a ghost of a
chance.
     Banquo at your
banquet   or   Hamlet's
father   embarrassing
everyone.
      I persist.

LIV

He says   remember
me? Wolf Creek? My
past smacks into my
present   in her
living room   but
why were we there or
here for that matter?

LV

Cross out desire.
Such complications   she said

not on my agenda.
        I
need my isolation to work
sacrifice warmth for
steely intellect
pour onto paper
fleshly caresses
meant for your
skin.
        My muse
reaches up her arms for
me   holds me tightly
while I continue to put down
words   one at a time
wondering if this is a
trap too.
        Outside the
inconstant sun   dis
appears in fog   my
lover will not warm me this
morning.

LVI

By Thanksgiving there is
snow in Pennsylvania.
                A
circular telling   a
spiraling
down.
        I can't
believe you have stopped
writing or loving
me.
        I watch my
friends going on

journeys   they do not
want to.
         They tell me
they are sick or injured.
Cannot see how they can
do this   yet do.
         I watch
in wonder at such
will.   Why not stay home?
I say   surely these are
messages.
         Bodies that resent
decisions   made only by the
mind   would keep you
here.
         But no they say
will   will   will   will
will take me there.

LVII

Gradually   another branch
dies on the avocado
tree   and nothing new
appears.
         Yes
you can still make my
heart beat fast when I
think of you.
         I am not
over you. Not yet.

LVIII

The sun   burns into my

head   through the glass
leaving its cancer rays
outside.

LVIX

I do not accept the
wise woman. I say   I am
not crone.
        Age is no
passport to that
country.

LX

I gave you back to
yourself.
        Did not steal your
image   but asked
permission.
        Did not keep
any.
        No piece of your
soul.

LXI

        The painting
grows daily   in my
head   southwest   color
black form   glowing red
eyes   turquoise sky.
        When
will I begin?
        This is the
time for prayer.

LXII

Once I gave you a scarf
silk in black and gold
hand painted.
            I
did not buy myself
one. I could not
afford two.
            An
expensive gift for a
friend   more like
a lover's gift.
            And
though I denied it
even to myself   that's
what it was   even though
you said   friend
friend.

LXIII

How many of us
are descendants from
rape?
        From invasions of
women's bodies?
        Mixing the
blood of many
tribes.
        Is this how
we become
one?

LXIV

Question:
        Why are

people destroying
themselves?
      Answer:
Because we don't need
them.

LXV

      Wrap me in a
cradle of rain
song.

LXVI

      Alone in this
time of change   this
changing time.
      Each of
us standing on the
edge   wondering
surrounded by
domestic shadows
children abused by
fathers   women raped by
men   children   killing
children.
      Men   women
children learning to live
without homes.

LXVII

      I am afraid of
guns.
      If I owned
one   I would want to
use it.

182

I always
play with my new
toy.
My tape
recorder   my VCR   my
computer   my
gun?

LXVIII

Boundaries are
melting.
Who today
knows   right   from
wrong?
Right is
turned on its
head.
Wrong
way   wrong way.

LXIX

Cut off my right
arm   or my left
I would be as
confused   no
longer   knowing
where you live   or
I.
My memory
now lost to me
that faithful dog
trotting in circles
looking for your
home   your

phone number on a
scrap   you no longer   you
no linger   except
I remember.

LXX

Driving home she
missed the explosion by
five minutes.
          The
mailbox   blown
across the road   the
metal flag   driven
into a young tree
trunk   the
bomb   demolishing its
container.

LXXI

        It was full
moon.   She was walking her
dog. I was leaving my
studio.
        We met electric
in the night.

LXXII

        The sea is at my
back   several miles   away.
We all know a tsunami
would wipe us away   a three
foot wall of water would
slice us or crush us.

          We all
know and we go on living
here.
          We do not even make
plans   as we do for
earthquakes.
          We live on the
Bottoms   people have
farmed here for years.
          Blue
eyed seacoast people.
          Mountain
people find it difficult to understand
such bravado   indifference
but really we forget.
          That both protects
us and puts us in danger.
          You
live in the center of this
country   no earthquakes
no tsunamis   no tornadoes.
          Once
you lived here   next to
danger.
          Is that why you never
came back?

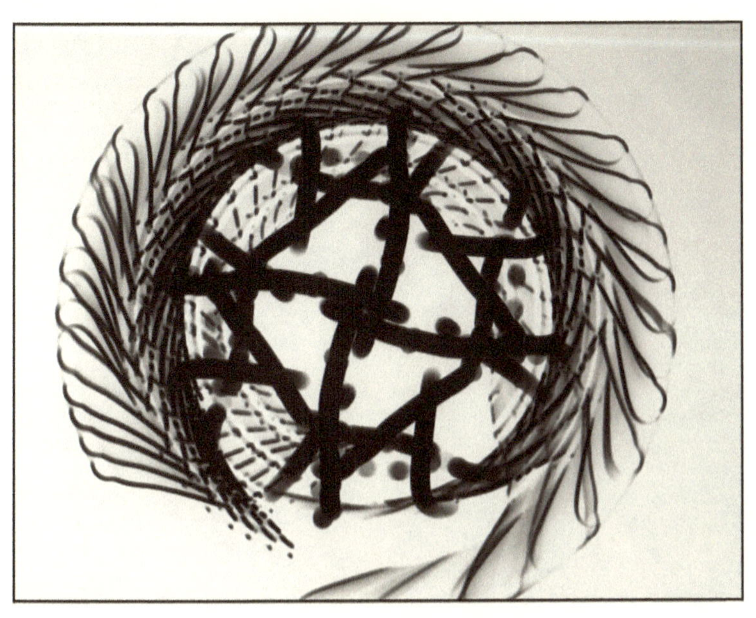

About the Editors,
Vincent Peloso & Sue Hilton

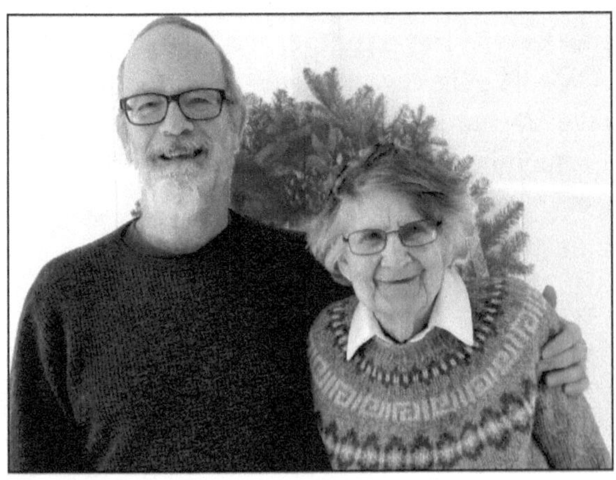

A New Jersey native, Vincent "Vinnie" Peloso earned a B.Ed. and M.Ed. from the University of Massachusetts before relocating to California where he worked as a minimum wage/tipped employee for 22 years while writing, reading and studying poetry in his spare time. He retired from a tenured faculty position teaching Reading and General Studies at the College of the Redwoods in Eureka, California in 2016.

From 1994 to 1999, he co-hosted the "Poets at the Jam" reading series at the Jambalaya Club in Arcata, California. In 1999, Vincent led the Bus Poster Project under the direction of The Ink People Center for the Arts, in cooperation with the Redwood Transit Authority. From 1994 to 2008, he produced and hosted the "Mad River Anthology," a twice monthly poetry program on KHSU radio.

Vincent attended the Community of Writers Conference in Olympic Valley, California, the Port Townsend Writers Conference, the Summer Arts Festival at Humboldt State University, the Mendocino Writers Conference, the North Coast Redwoods Writers Conference and the Colrain Manuscript Conference.

A manuscript of his work was the first runner-up for the 2012 Bordighera Poetry Prize. Another was a finalist in the 2016 Concrete Wolf Louis Award. Over the years, dozens of his poems have appeared in dozens of small journals. He is currently a member of the Lost Coast Writers Community which meets annually in Petrolia, California.

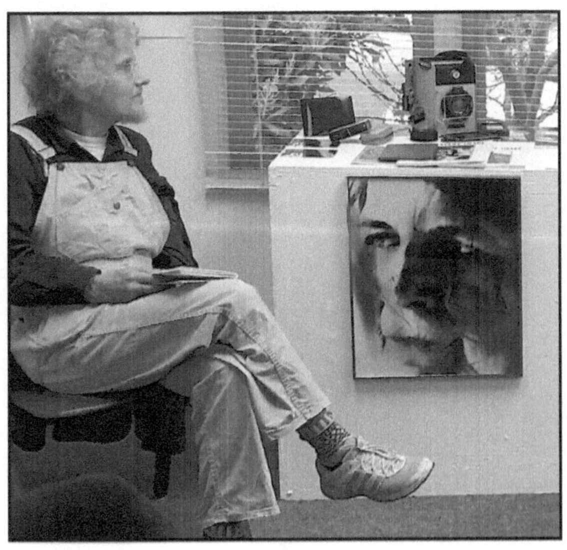

Sue Hilton was raised in Michigan's Upper Peninsula, and spends her working life in forests and creeks, mostly in Northern California. When she's not exploring woods and water she agitates against war and for women, queers, justice, and the planet. She lives in Arcata, California, where she is the editor of the *L-Word*, a Humboldt County monthly lesbian/queer newsletter, now in its 37th year.

As the *L-Word* editor, Sue published five chapbooks (2010-2020) called *Poetry from the Edge of the Continent: Poetry by Readers, Writers and Friends of the* L-Word, initially edited by Barb Dilworth and Deborah Carroll, and later by Sue. With Ruth Mountaingrove and Renee Rawski, Sue produced a chapbook of local photographs and Humboldt Bay poems by Barbara Dilworth, *Water Meeting Water*. Sue edited and published Ruth's second poetry collection, *I Remind Myself*, in 2015.

About the Publisher

"I believe the true identity is found in creative activity springing from within."—Writer & Pioneering Aviator, Anne Morrow Lindbergh 1906-2001

Kate Hitt established Many Names Press Printing and Publishing around 1996 for her literary and artistic friends and relatives to broadcast their exemplary works. Since then she has published over 30 fine art, poetry and prose books.

After working in the print and copy industry in Arcata, California, (1979-1986,) she moved to the Monterey Bay Area and Santa Cruz, where, in addition to offset press printing and letterpress, she learned fine hand bookbinding, rare book collecting, digital imaging, layout formatting, editing, graphics and book design. She retired from her day job driving the big yellow schoolbus after almost 14 years, and returned to Humboldt in late 2019.

An avid reader and writer since she was a kid living in Rome, Italy, Kate is also a poet and visual artist. She holds a degree in Comparative Literature from the University of Virginia, which has been very useful for publishing books and living a thoughtful, creative life.

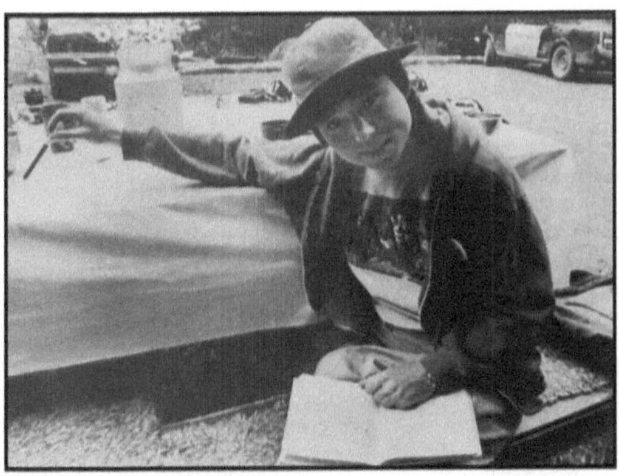

Ovular, 1983, Writing for The Blatant Image.
Photo by Janice Baker

Colophon

Many Names Press
believes in the power of published literature:
to foster respect for women & children everywhere,
to overcome injustice & warring minds,
to develop work parity and equality,
to support, nurture & protect
this world
for all beings.

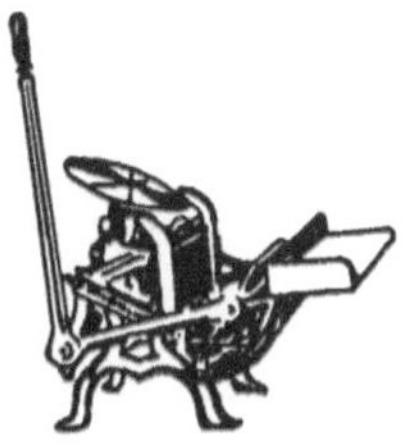

This book uses the fonts Calligraphic 421 for the titling,
and Goudy Old Style for the body of text.

Typographer Brian Coale said, *Elegant and stately, Goudy
Old Style is a fine choice for any creative that requires an
ambiance of beauty and nobility.*